How to Study

25th Anniversary Edition

How to Study

The Program That Has
Helped Millions of Students
Study Smarter, Not Harder

RON FRY

The Career Press, Inc.
Wayne, NJ

HOW TO STUDY
TYPESET BY KRISTIN GOBLE
COVER ILLUSTRATION BY VLADGRIN/SHUTTERSTOCK
Printed in the U.S.A.

To order this title, please call toll-free 1-800-CAREER-1 (NJ and Canada: 201-848-0310) to order using VISA or MasterCard, or for further information on books from Career Press.

B CAREER
PRESS

The Career Press, Inc.
12 Parish Drive
Wayne, NJ 07470
www.careerpress.com

Library of Congress Cataloging-in-Publication Data

CIP Data Available Upon Request.

TABLE OF CONTENTS

Introduction

Study to Succeed

"Learning is its own exceeding great reward."
—William Hazlitt

As I began preparing this new edition, I wasn't sure how drastically I would need to change it. Had technology—from SMARTBoards and smart phones to a million apps and a zillion Websites—so altered the educational landscape that many of the study tips and techniques I'd written about were obsolete?

Thinking about all of the technological changes that have occurred in the last decade spurred me to rethink every aspect of this book. Were there now easier or more efficient ways to accomplish the same age-old study tasks? Were there new problems that had to be addressed? Were there suggestions or tools that were now hopelessly out of date?

Since, as Montaigne declared, "a man must always study," I am happy to report that today's successful student needs to master the same basic set of study skills. However, the most efficient ways to master them and, especially, the variety of tools available to do so, clearly have grown and evolved.

So this edition of *How to Study* still includes hints, advice, and techniques for reading, understanding, and remembering what you read; taking notes in class, from your textbooks, in the library, and online; how to prepare for and do better on all kinds of tests; how to research and prepare great papers and oral reports; and how to organize your study schedule to get the best results in the shortest amount of time. But there are essential skills you may think have nothing to do with studying, and important steps you need to take right from the start, that we will cover first.

Here's where to start

> "Learning without thought is labor lost. Thought without learning is perilous."
>
> —Confucius

Developing great study habits is like a footrace between you and your friends. Before you can declare a winner, you have to agree on where the finish line is. In other words, how do you measure your ability to use these skills? What's a good result? What's a poor one?

But you can't even start the race until you know where the *starting* line is—especially if it's drawn at a different spot for each of you!

Chapter 1 starts by explaining each study skill and clarifying how each can and should function in your life. Then you'll be given the chance to identify your own starting line.

In Chapter 2, you'll learn the importance of where, how, and when you study, and you will start building the study environment that's perfect for *you.*

There is no magic elixir in the study habit regimen. If math and science are not your strong suits, memorizing *How to Study* will not transform you into a Nobel Prize-winning physicist. Nobody is great at *every*thing, but everybody is great at *some*thing. So you'll also get a chance to rate the subjects you like and dislike, and those that are your best and worst.

Chapter 2 also introduces some of the "intangibles" in the study equation: your home environment, attitude, motivation, and so forth. If you are dedicated to studying and motivated to achieve certain goals, all the other factors that affect your study habits will fall more naturally into place. A belief in the study ethic is one of the keys to success.

Finally, mastering some other key components of the study process—learning to "read" teachers, developing mentors, dealing with perfectionism, the importance of flexibility—will help you get off to the right start.

Reading and comprehension

Chapter 3 introduces the skills basic to any study process: reading and comprehension. No matter how well you learn to take notes, how familiar you become with your library, how deftly you operate online, and how doggedly you study for tests, if you are reading poorly (or not enough) and not understanding or remembering what you read, life will be difficult.

Becoming a good reader is a skill, one usually acquired early in life. If it's a skill you haven't acquired yet, now is the time!

Maximize your memory

In Chapter 4, I have reintroduced memory tips, tricks and techniques that were eliminated in earlier editions to keep this book at a manageable length. But I think learning how to remember numbers, memorize long lists, create "chain-link" stories, and other essential memory techniques are too important to leave out. I have also moved some of the material previously included in Chapter 3—how to remember more of what you read—into this new chapter.

Making up for lost time

To see a significant change in your life, many of you will not need to study *harder,* just *smarter.* This means making better use of your study time—spending the same two, three or four hours, but accomplishing twice, thrice, or four times as much. Chapter 5 introduces a number of simple and easy-to-use organizational and time-management tools—powerful ways to make sure you are always on track and on time.

Go to the head of the class

In Chapter 6, I talk about the one experience we all have in common, no matter how old we are: the classroom. I'll help you take better notes in every kind of classroom, encourage your active participation in class discussions, and help you get a lot more out of lectures.

Create a great term paper

In early editions of this book, I included a chapter on using your library, later changed to "How to Conduct Your Research" so as to incorporate the now far-more-prevalent use of online resources. It was a relatively short chapter followed by a far longer one detailing all the other steps necessary to produce a terrific essay, term paper, or oral report.

In this edition, I have rearranged these two chapters so they are more equal in length. So Chapter 7 now covers all the preparatory steps to complete any writing assignment, from choosing a topic and establishing a long-term schedule to establishing an initial thesis, creating a rough outline and conducting research, in the library and/or online.

I still briefly review the two major library classification systems—Dewey Decimal and Library of Congress—and show you how to conduct efficient online research without falling prey—for hours—to the "let's-just-follow-that-interesting-link" syndrome.

Chapter 8 now assumes most if not all of your research has been completed and takes you through the actual organizational and writing processes, from creating your first draft through rewriting, proofreading, and finalizing footnotes, to the appendices and the bibliography. It also includes a brief section on the key differences between producing a written report and presenting the same information orally.

How to ace any test

Chapter 9 covers the do's and don'ts of test preparation, including the differences between studying for weekly quizzes, midterms, and final examinations; why last-minute cramming doesn't work (but how to do it if you have no choice—shame!); studying for and taking different types of tests (multiple choice, true-false, essay, open book, and so on); how to increase your guessing scores; even which questions to answer first and which to leave for last.

How smart do *you* study?

How to Study is the most comprehensive study guide ever written—a fundamental, step-by-step approach that anyone can follow to develop and sharpen his or her study skills.

If you're struggling through college or graduate school, here's your life preserver.

If you're a high school student planning to attend college, *now*'s your chance to hone your study skills.

If you're not considering college—even if you're ready to drop out of high school at the earliest possible opportunity— you still need *How to Study*.

If you're an adult returning to the classroom after a lengthy absence, there's no substitute for the tips and techniques you will learn in this book.

What if you're a really poor student? How smart you are is not the point. *What counts is how smart you study.*

With the possible exception of the two percent of you who qualify as "gifted," *How to Study* will help students of any age and ability level.

If your grades are average to good, you will see a definite improvement. If you are barely passing, you will benefit considerably. If good study habits are in place but rusty as a result of years away from the classroom, *How to Study* will be the perfect refresher for you.

And if you *are* one of those "gifted" two percent, I *still* think you'll find many helpful techniques in these pages.

Who is this book really for?

Although I originally wrote *How to Study* for high school students, I've discovered over the years that many more audiences have benefited from it.

The surprise was that so many of the people buying *How to Study* were adults. Yes, a number of them were returning to school and saw *How to Study* as a great refresher. And some were long out of school but had figured out that if they could learn *now* the study skills their teachers never taught them (or they never took the time to learn), they would do better in their careers.

All too many were parents who had the same lament: "How do I get Johnny to read (show up on time, remember more, get better grades)?"

So I want to briefly take the time to address every one of the audiences for this book and discuss some of the factors particular to each of you.

If you're a high school student

You should be particularly comfortable with the format of the book: its relatively short sentences and paragraphs, occasionally humorous (hopefully) headings and subheadings, and the language used. I *did* originally write it with you in mind!

But you should also be *un*comfortable with the fact that you're already in the middle of your school years—the period that will drastically affect, one way or the other, all the *rest* of your school years—*and you still don't know how to study!* Don't lose another minute: Make learning how to study and mastering *all* of the study skills in this book your *absolute priority.*

If you're a middle school student

Congratulations! You're learning how to study at *precisely* the right time. Sixth, seventh, and eighth grades—before that sometimes-cosmic leap to high school—is without a doubt the period in which all these study skills should be mastered.

Doing so will make high school not just easier but a far more positive and successful experience.

If you're a "traditional" college student

If you are somewhere in the 18 to 25 age range, I hope you are tackling one or two of the study skills you failed to master in high school. If you are deficient in more areas than that and fail to address all of them, I can't see how you're ever going to succeed in college. (Then again, I can't figure out how you managed to get *into* college.) If you are starting from scratch, my advice is the same as to the high school students reading this book: Make learning how to study your top priority.

If you're a nontraditional student

If you're going back to high school, college, or graduate school at age 25, 45, 65, or 85, you probably need the help in *How to Study* more than anyone! The longer you've been out of school, the more likely you don't remember what you've forgotten. And you've forgotten what you're supposed to remember! As much as I emphasize that it's rarely too early to learn good study habits, I must also emphasize that it's never too *late*.

What can parents do?

"Education, like neurosis, begins at home."
—Milton Sapirstein

There are probably even more dedicated parents out there than dedicated students, since the first phone call at any of my radio or TV appearances inevitably comes from a sincere and worried parent asking, "What can I do to help my kid do better in school?" Here are the rules for parents of students of any age:

> **Set up a homework area.** Free of distraction, well-lit, with all necessary supplies handy.

> **Set up a homework routine.** Studies have clearly shown that students who establish a regular routine are better organized and, as a result, more successful.

> **Set homework priorities.** Actually, just make the point that homework *is* the priority—before a date, before TV, before going out to play, whatever.

> **Make reading a habit.** For them, certainly, but also for yourselves. Kids will inevitably do what you *do*, not what you *say* (even if you say *not* to do what you do). So if you keep nagging them to read while you settle in for a 24-hour *Breaking Bad* marathon, please consider the mixed message you are sending.

> **Turn off the TV.** Or, at the very least, severely limit when and how much TV-watching is appropriate. This may be the toughest suggestion to implement—I know, I weathered the *sturm* and *drang* of my daughter's teen-aged years.

> **Talk to the teachers.** Find out what your kids are supposed to be learning. How else will you know what help they need? You may even be "helping" them in ways that are at odds with what the teacher is trying to accomplish.

> **Encourage and motivate**, but don't nag them to do their homework. It doesn't work. The more you insist, the quicker they will tune you out.

> **Supervise their work**, but don't fall into the trap of *doing* their homework for them. Proofreading a paper, for example, is a positive way to help your child in school. But if you then enter all the corrections yourself, your child has learned nothing...except that she is not responsible for her own work.

> **Praise them when they succeed**, but don't overpraise them for mediocre work. Kids have well-attuned antennae for insincerity.

> **Convince older students of reality.** Learning and believing that the real world won't care about their grades, but will measure them by what they know and what they can do, is a lesson that will save many tears (probably yours). It's probably never too early to (carefully and tenderly) inform your little genius that life really isn't fair...and give him or her the resources to help deal with that fact.

> **Make sure your kids have the technology they need to succeed.** Whatever their age, your kids really must be computer savvy and have Internet access in order to survive in and after school.

> **Turn off the TV already!**

> **Hide their cellphone and turn off IM (Instant Messaging) and text alerts** while they are doing homework. They will inevitably try to convince you that texts, chats, alerts, and messages will in no way interfere with their algebra homework. Parents who buy this argument have also been persuaded that sitting in front of the TV is the best place to study.

Are you ready to learn something?

The book you are holding in your hands (or on your E-reader) is now in its eighth edition and has been helping students and parents (and even teachers) for more than 25 years. If you need even more help in a particular area, there are five other specific titles in *Ron Fry's How to Study Program: "Ace" Any Test, Get Organized, Improve Your Memory, Improve Your Reading,* and *Improve Your Writing.*

Thank you for making all of these books successful.

Learning shouldn't be painful or boring, though it is occasionally both. I don't promise that *How to Study* will make *everything* easier. It won't. It can't. And it may actually require some work to achieve what you want. But *How to Study will* illuminate the path, give you directions, and make sure you're properly provisioned for your journey.

In some classes, you will not understand everything the first time you read it or hear it. Or, perhaps, even the second or third time. You may have to learn it slowly, very slowly. But that doesn't mean there's something wrong with you. It may be a subject that *everyone* learns slowly. (My particular nemesis was Physical Chemistry.) A poorly written textbook or unmotivated teacher can make any subject difficult.

You will also inevitably decide that one or more courses couldn't possibly be of any use later in life. "I don't have a clue why I need to learn trigonometry (physics, French literature, European history, fill in the blank)," you wail. "I will *never* use it."

Believe me, you have no idea what you may or may not need, use or remember next *week,* let alone in a decade. In my experience, a surprising amount of "useless" information and learning wound up being vitally important to my professional career.

So learn it all. Get excited about the *process* of learning, and I guarantee you will not ever worry about what you will need to know in the future.

I immodestly maintain that *How to Study* is the best book on the market. There are certainly lots of other study books out there. Unfortunately, I don't think many of them deliver what they promise.

The author of one such title spent barely half a dozen pages on time management...and 26 pages discussing the importance of sleep, exercise, and nutrition (including sample menus).

I see little reason to waste your time detailing what should be obvious: Anything—including studying—is more difficult if you're tired, hungry, unhealthy, drunk, stoned, and so on. So please use common sense. Eat as healthily as you can, get whatever sleep your body requires, stay reasonably fit, and avoid alcohol and drugs. If your lack of success is in any way due to one of these other factors and you're unable to deal with it alone, find a good book or a professional to help you.

Another author posed some basic questions: "When should I study?" "Where should I study?" "How long should I study?" He then provided his absolute answers: "Early," "in isolation," and "no more than an hour at a time."

As far as I am concerned, there are few "rights" and "wrongs" out there in the study world. There's certainly no single "right" way to attack a multiple choice test or absolute "right" way to take notes. So don't get fooled into thinking there *is*, especially if what you're doing seems to be working for you. Don't change what "ain't broke" just because some self-proclaimed study guru claims what you're doing is all wet. Maybe she's all wet.

Needless to say, don't read *my* books looking for some single, inestimable system of "rules" that works for everyone.

You won't find it, 'cause there's no such bird. You *will* find a plethora of techniques, tips, tricks, gimmicks, and what-have-yous, some or all of which will work for you, some of which won't. Pick and choose, change and adapt, figure out what works for you—because *you* are responsible for creating *your* study system, *not me*.

I think we've spent enough time talking about what you're *going* to learn. Let's get on with the learning.

—Ron Fry

Chapter 1

Start off Right

"Learn what you are and be such."

—Pindar

In the next two chapters, I'm going to help you:

> Evaluate the current level of all your study skills so you can identify those areas in which you need to concentrate your efforts;

> Identify the study environment and learning style that suit you; and

> Categorize all of your school subjects according to how well you *like* them and how well you *do* in them.

How to keep score

In the next few pages, I'll explain the primary study skills covered in this book: reading and comprehension; memory development; time management; note-taking (in your textbooks, in class, in the library, while online); classroom participation; researching and writing papers; and test preparation. Then I'll ask you to rate yourself on your current level of achievement and understanding of each: "A" (excellent) for mastery or near mastery of a particular skill; "B" (good) for some mastery; C (fair to poor) for little or no mastery.

But let's do a general test first, just to give you a taste of what's to come. Read the following 28 statements and consider which apply to you. If a statement does apply, mark "Y" (for yes). If not, mark "N" (for no):

1. ___Y ___N I wish I could read faster.
2. ___Y ___N I go to class, but I don't pay a lot of attention.
3. ___Y ___N I rarely review for tests, but I do spend hours cramming the night before.
4. ___Y ___N I think I spend more time studying than I need to.
5. ___Y ___N I usually study with the TV on and constantly check my cellphone.
6. ___Y ___N I rarely finish all my homework on time.
7. ___Y ___N I usually write assigned papers the week (or the night) before they're due.
8. ___Y ___N I read every book at the same speed and in the same way.
9. ___Y ___N I can never seem to find the information I need on the Internet.

10. ___Y ___N   I'm overwhelmed with too much homework.

11. ___Y ___N   I can never complete my reading assignments on time.

12. ___Y ___N   I always seem to write down the wrong stuff in class.

13. ___Y ___N   I frequently forget important assignments and test dates.

14. ___Y ___N   I get nervous before exams and do worse than I think I should.

15. ___Y ___N   I frequently must reread whole passages two or three times before I understand them.

16. ___Y ___N   When I finish reading a chapter, I usually don't remember much of it.

17. ___Y ___N   I try to take down everything the teacher says but usually can't understand any of my notes.

18. ___Y ___N   I can only study for about 15 minutes before I get bored or distracted.

19. ___Y ___N   When I'm working on a paper or report, I spend most of the time with a thesaurus in my lap.

20. ___Y ___N   I always seem to study the wrong stuff.

21. ___Y ___N   I don't use any kind of calendar.

22. ___Y ___N   I study for some tests, but I always forget what I studied when I get there.

23. ___Y ___N   I don't have enough time to do well in school and still have a social life.

24. ___Y ___N   I can't figure out the important points in my textbooks.

25. ___Y ___N When I look at my class notes right
             before a test, I can't understand them.
26. ___Y ___N I hate to read.
27. ___Y ___N I get marked down on essay tests
             because I don't organize them well.
28. ___Y ___N I spend a lot of time on my computer but
             it feels like most of it is wasted.

What do your answers mean? If you answered "yes" to questions:

> 2, 5, or 18, you need to work on your
  concentration.
> 1, 8, 15, 16, 24, or 26, your reading and compre-
  hension skills are holding you back.
> 3, 14, or 22, you need to learn the proper way to
  study for tests and how to reduce test anxiety.
> 4, 6, 10, 11, 13, 21, or 23, your organizational
  skills are letting you down.
> 7, 19, or 27, you're spending a lot of time "writ-
  ing" papers but haven't learned how to properly
  research or organize them.
> 9 or 28, you need to hone your computer skills
  and learn how to efficiently identify pertinent
  information online.
> 12, 17, 20, or 25, you need a better system for
  taking notes in class and from your textbooks.

It's not as important how *many* "yes" answers you had
as it is how many were grouped in a specific area—the one
in which you obviously need help. (Though 10 or more "yes"
answers would indicate problems in more than a single area.)

Let's go into a little more detail and get an even firmer
handle on the current state of your study skills. I've listed
the primary study skills on page 25. Take a separate piece of

paper and rate yourself on each of them (from reading and comprehension through test preparation) *before you read the rest of this chapter.* Then give yourself two points for every A, one point for every B, and zero points for every C.

If your overall rating is 17 or more, give yourself an A on the "Initial self-evaluation" line; 13 to 16, give yourself a B; and if 12 or less, give yourself a C. This is your assessment of your study habits as they exist right now.

Now, let's review each of these areas and get a better understanding of what "excellent," "good," and "fair" really mean. As you read each section, fill in your rating on the "Your Starting Point" chart—and be honest with yourself. This evaluation will give you a benchmark from which to measure your improvement after you've finished *How to Study.* File it away and make the comparison when you've completed reading.

Remember: There are no right or wrong answers in either of these assessments. They are jumping-off points from which you can measure your progress and identify those areas in which your skills need improvement.

Your Starting Point

Initial self-evaulation	A ( ) B ( ) C ( )	
Reading & comprehension	A ( ) B ( ) C ( )	
Memory development	A ( ) B ( ) C ( )	
Time management	A ( ) B ( ) C ( )	
Textbook note-taking	A ( ) B ( ) C ( )	
Taking notes in class	A ( ) B ( ) C ( )	
Library note-taking	A ( ) B ( ) C ( )	
Taking notes online	A ( ) B ( ) C ( )	
Classroom participation	A ( ) B ( ) C ( )	
Writing papers	A ( ) B ( ) C ( )	
Test preparation	A ( ) B ( ) C ( )	
Overall study skill level	A ( ) B ( ) C ( )	

Reading and comprehension

Speed, comprehension, and recall are the three important components of reading. Comprehension and recall are especially interrelated—better to sacrifice some speed to increase these two factors. To test your reading and comprehension skills, read the passage below (excerpted from *U.S. History: From Reconstruction Through the Dawn of the 21st Century* by Ron Olson). Then close the book, jot down the key points made in the selection you read, review the text, and compare your notes with the reading selection. You will get a good idea of how well you understood what you read and just how good your "top-of-the-mind" recall is.

World War I left many Americans disillusioned about war, and the United States retreated into isolationism. Britain and France began to acquiesce to the demands of a new aggressor: Adolph Hitler. Indifference about the changing nation-states in Europe and appeasement of aggressors had ultimately led to global violence. By the late 1930s, 70 percent of Americans felt that the role the country had played in World War I was a mistake.

The United States passed Neutrality Acts allowing it to deny the sale or shipment of munitions to warring nations, opting instead for a cash-and-carry policy. The country needed the income, but it was unwilling to commit to another war. The rumblings of conflict frightened many as totalitarian leaders across the globe flexed their muscles. These leaders posed a threat to security, and the United States couldn't ignore the possibility of involvement in yet another global conflict. The deaths of 50 million people, along with the horrors and destruction of war, provided a stark conclusion to the conflict of World War II. The devastating loss of population and property in Europe and Japan, the Holocaust that killed six million Jews, the development and use of the atomic bomb, the Soviet domination of Eastern Europe, a divided Germany, Japanese internment camps, and the founding of the United Nations made this war far different from any other in history.

Isolationism was no longer possible. In the United States, World War II highlighted racial inequalities, gave women new opportunities, and fostered growth in the South and West. By devastating the nation's commercial rivals, World War II left the United States dominant in the world economy. It also increased the scope of the federal government and built an alliance among the armed forces, big business, and science that helped shape post-war America.

Score: If you can read the material straight through, accurately summarize what you've read, even remember key names and statistics, all in less than two minutes, award yourself an A. If you have some problems reading and understanding the text but are able to complete the assignment in less than four minutes, give yourself a B. If you are unable to complete the assignment in that time, remember what you read, or produce accurate notes at all, give yourself a C.

Memory development

Test #1: Look at the number following this paragraph for 10 seconds. Then cover the page and write down as much of it as you can remember:

762049582049736

Score: If you remembered 12 or more digits in the correct order, give yourself an A; eight to 11, a B; seven or less, a C.

Test #2: Below are 12 nonsense words from a language I just made up and their "definitions." Study the list for 60 seconds and try to remember each word, how it's spelled, and its definition:

Capulam	tea cup	Maghor	a rice dish
Armarek	curtain	Jerysh	armband
Zynder	to hum	Opockal	secure
Thromph	necklace	Stapnor	nurse
Booleric	snack	Yeffer	to dunk
Cwassul	paper sack	Fravitous	hungry

Done? Close the book and write down each of the 12 words and its definition. They do not need to be in the order in which they were listed.

Score: If you accurately listed nine or more words and definitions (and that includes spelling my new words correctly), give yourself an A. If you listed from five to eight words and their definitions, or correctly listed and spelled nine or more words but mixed up their definitions, give yourself a B. If you were unable to remember at least four words and their definitions, give yourself a C.

Test #3: Here's a list of real Egyptian pharaohs in the order of their reigns:

Narmer	Anedjib
Hor-aha	Semerkhet
Djer	Qu'a
Djet	Sneferka
Merneith	Horus Bird
Den	Hotepsekhemwy

Can you create a visual, chain-link story in less than three minutes that would allow you to easily remember them, spelled correctly and in order?

Score: If you created a story, no matter how strange, that enabled you to correctly spell the names of at least nine of the 12 pharaohs and listed them in order, give yourself an A. Six to eight, give yourself a B. Five or less, give yourself a C. (I will admit that Hotepsekhemwy is a mouthful, but I gave you Djer, Djet, Den, and Qu'a, didn't I?)

Time management

Your effective use of available study time can be measured by two yardsticks: (1) your ability to break down assignments into component parts (for example, reading, note taking, outlining, writing); and (2) your ability to complete each task in an efficient manner.

Score: If you feel you use your time wisely and efficiently, give yourself an A. If you know there *are* times you simply run out of time, give yourself a B. If you can't *tell* time, give yourself a C.

Taking clear and effective notes

Four different arenas—at home with your textbooks, in the classroom, at the library, and online—require different methods of note taking.

From your textbooks: Working from your books at home, you should identify the main ideas, rephrase information in your own words, and capture unfamiliar details. As you read, take brief, concise notes in a separate notebook or the text's margins or highlight/underline pertinent information in the text. You should write down questions and answers to ensure your mastery of the material, starring those questions for which you *don't* have answers so you can ask them in class.

In class: Class *preparation* is the key to class *participation*. By reading material to be covered before class, you will be able to concentrate and absorb the teacher's interpretations and points. Using a topical, short-sentence approach or your own shorthand or symbols, take notes on those items that will help you remember and recall the subject matter. Your notes should be sequential, following the teacher's lecture pattern. Review your notes at the first opportunity following class. Fill in any blanks and add your own thoughts.

In the library and online: What's the difference between taking notes at the library, from your textbooks and online? Sooner or later you'll have to return library books (if you're allowed to take them out at all), and librarians tend to frown on highlighting them. And unless you plan to print out every Web page you find and wield your magic highlighter, you need an effective system for taking notes right from the source, whether it's a library book, journal article, or Web page.

Of course, if you are so unfamiliar with your public or school library that you don't even know its address, you will have a hard time utilizing its offerings when a paper is assigned.

Likewise, if your idea of efficient use of the Internet is staying up-to-date on Kylie Jenner's latest musings and making sure to post on Instagram every hour on the hour, you will find researching a 15-page paper on Japanese internment camps during World War II, uh, challenging.

Score: Are your note-taking skills sufficient to summarize the necessary data from your textbooks?

Are you able to capture the key points from classroom lectures and discussions?

Are you such a ubiquitous presence in your library that they have named a study carrel for you?

Are you able to find a dozen key Internet sites pertinent to any paper within minutes?

If your note-taking skills allow you to master your textbooks, excel in class, find whatever information you need from a variety of sources, prepare detailed outlines, and write good papers, give yourself an A in each area. If you feel you are deficient in any one of these areas of note taking, give yourself a B. If notes are what you pass to your friends in class, give yourself a C.

Class participation

Most teachers take each student's class participation into account when calculating final grades, no matter how many pop quizzes they pull or how many term papers they assign. And, you may have discovered, there are teachers who will mark down even those students who "ace" every paper and quiz if they seem to disappear in the classroom.

Score: If you are always prepared for class (which means, at the very least, reading all assigned material, preparing assigned homework and projects, and turning them in on time), actively participate in discussions, and ask frequent and pertinent questions as a way of both trumpeting what you already know and filling in the gaps in that knowledge, give yourself an A. If you fail in any of these criteria, give yourself a B. If you aren't sure where the classroom is, give yourself a C.

Writing papers and preparing oral reports

With apologies to Thomas Edison, preparing any sort of report, written or oral, is 90 percent perspiration (research) and 10 percent inspiration (writing). In other words, the ability to write a good paper is more dependent on your mastery of the other skills we've already discussed than your mastery of *writing.* If you are an avid reader, familiar with your local library, a veteran online researcher, a good note-taker, and capable of breaking down the most complex topic into the manageable steps necessary to write a paper, you probably turn in superior papers.

Score: If you have already given yourself an A in library and online note taking, time management, and reading, give yourself an A. If you feel you turn in relatively good papers but definitely lack in any of these areas, give yourself a B. If your idea of writing a paper is photocopying the pertinent *Spark Notes* and retyping the summary, give yourself a C.

Test preparation

The key to proper test preparation is knowing both what material will be covered and what form the test will take.

Weekly quizzes or unit/chapter exams usually cover the most recent material. Midterms and finals cover a much broader area—usually all the subject matter to date. Multiple-choice tests, essays, lists of math problems, and science lab tests all require different preparation and apply different test-taking skills.

Knowing the kind of test you're facing will make your preparation much easier. So will creating a list of questions you think your teacher will most likely ask. By periodically reviewing your text and class notes, you'll begin to identify the areas in which your teacher appears most interested...and on which he or she is most likely to test you. As a final trick, prepare a list of 10 or more questions *you* would ask if *you* were the teacher.

Score: If you are able to construct tests that are harder than the ones your teacher gives you—and score well on his or hers—give yourself an A. If you feel you know the material, but just don't perform as well as you think you should at test time, give yourself a B. If you didn't pass your driver's test, let alone algebra, give yourself a C.

Your overall score

Once again, after you've rated yourself in each area, give yourself two points for every A, one point for every B, and zero points for every C. If your overall rating is 17 or more, excellent (give yourself an A); 13 to 16, good (give yourself a B); 12 or less, fair (give yourself a C). Put your new score in the section "Overall study skill level" in the chart on p. 25.

How closely did this more detailed evaluation compare with the score you gave yourself before reading the rest of this chapter? If the latter was wildly off the mark, it just means you aren't as ready to toss this book as you thought you were! If your initial evaluation wasn't as positive as the more detailed one you just completed, you're in better shape than you thought!

Now what?

The fact that you have been honest with yourself in evaluating the talents you bring to the study game is a big plus in your favor. Knowing your areas of strength and weakness, especially the skills you need to develop or improve, will help you concentrate your efforts.

Although I would strongly recommend you read the entire book, this simple test has enabled you to identify the chapters you really need to study and the specific skills that may require your continued attention long after you finish reading this book.

Chapter 2

Develop your Plan

"In order that knowledge be properly digested, it must have been swallowed with a good appetite."

—ANATOLE FRANCE

If you are failing every subject right now, I cannot promise that *How to Study* will miraculously transform you into an A student. Clearly something is very wrong or very lacking. But I *can* promise you that whatever your current grades and effort, you will undoubtedly experience a positive change if you put in the time to practice the skills in this book.

You may not need to spend more time studying. You may simply need to learn how to study more efficiently, to use your time more economically, to study *smarter*. You may actually be able to devote *less* time and get better results.

Learning of *any* kind takes discipline. And learning self-discipline is, to many of us, the most difficult task of all. But you absolutely can achieve better grades and more success if you put in the time to learn the lessons *How to Study* contains and, more importantly, practice and use them every day.

If you're currently doing little or nothing in the way of schoolwork, then you *are* going to have to devote more time and effort. How much more? Or even more generally, how long should you study? Until you get the results you want to achieve. The smarter you are and the more easily you learn and adapt the techniques in *How to Study*, the more likely you will be spending *less* time on your homework than before. But the further you need to go—from Ds to As rather than Bs to As—the more you need to learn and the longer you need to give yourself to learn it.

Don't get discouraged. You *will* see positive results surprisingly quickly.

Make study habit-forming

If you're doing poorly in school but spending a reasonable amount of time studying, you may have poor study habits. I don't know where or when you acquired them, but failure has, to some extent, become a habit.

Good news! Not only can *bad* habits be broken, but they can be replaced by *good* habits relatively easily. Here's your battle plan:

> ❯   It is much easier to *replace* a habit than to break it entirely. So don't attempt to stop poor study habits—just learn the good ones to substitute for them.

> Practice is the motor oil that lubricates any habit's engine. The more you do something, the more ingrained it becomes.

> Tell your friends and family of your intention to improve your study skills and do better in school. (This is a trick that works for *some* people, who find that the added pressure is just the motivation they need.)

> To make sure you get a "motivational jolt" from every accomplishment, resolve to chart every inch of your progress, even if, like Robert Frost, you have "miles to go before you sleep." You may want to set up a chart on your wall or in your phone on which you list "Today's Successes" *every day.*

Starting with the next chapter, everything in this book will concentrate on specific strategies useful for specific tasks—paper-writing, note-taking, test-taking, reading, and so forth. So this is probably the best place to discuss some overall study strategies that have little to do with any particular task but everything to do with your eventual study success.

Nothing happens overnight

Learning how to study is a long-term process. Once you undertake the journey, you will be surprised at the number of landmarks, pathways, side streets, and road signs you'll find. Even after you've transformed yourself into a better student than you'd ever hoped to be, you'll inevitably find another informative signpost, another detour to explore, another route to exciting possibilities.

Consider learning how to study a *lifelong process,* and be ready to modify whatever you're doing as you learn other methods.

This is especially important right from the start, as you consider your overall study strategies. How long should you study per night? How do you allocate time between subjects? How often do you schedule breaks? Your answers to these questions are going to vary considerably depending on how well you were doing before you read this book, how far you have to go, how interested you are in getting there, how involved you are in other activities, the time of day, your general health, and a host of other individual factors.

What's your study sequence? Hardest assignments first? Easiest? Longest? Shortest? Are you comfortable switching back and forth from one subject to another, or do you prefer to focus on a single assignment until it is finished?

What's your study strategy? Your high school history teacher may want you to memorize a series of Civil War battles, dates, and generals. Your college professor will expect a deeper understanding of the battles, how they related to the overall conduct of the war, and how they affected or were affected by what was occurring in the rest of the world. *Your teacher's emphasis will change the way you study.*

The tasks themselves may have a great effect on your schedule. When I sit down to plan out the chapter of a book, for example, I need a relatively long period of uninterrupted time—at least an hour, perhaps as long as three hours. That's sufficient time to put my notes in the order I want them and think through the entire chapter—writing transitions in my head, noting problem areas, and figuring out where I need an example or illustration. As a result, if I only had half an hour before a meeting or appointment, I wouldn't even attempt to start such a project.

What's the lesson in all of this? There is no ideal, no answer—certainly no "right" answer—to many of the questions I've posed. It's a point I will emphasize again and again: Figure out what works for you and keep doing it. If it later stops working or doesn't seem to be working as well, change it.

None of the study techniques discussed at such length in this book is carved in stone. You not only should feel free to adapt and shape and bend each of them to your own needs, you *must* do so.

Select one from Column A...

A key way to ensure you don't fail a test before it even begins is to read the instructions. This will help you avoid the poor grade (not to mention the frustration and embarrassment) that will result from futilely trying to answer all six essay questions in an hour...when you were only supposed to answer three.

Tests aren't the only time "reading the instructions" is important. Many teachers have their own rules and regulations about turning in homework assignments, preparing papers or projects, reporting lab results, and so on. And it's just as important to follow *their* instructions—and just as devastating if you *don't*.

I really did have a teacher in 10th grade—when none of us had access to personal computers and few of us had learned to type—who failed a student because her paper was handwritten. What bothered me then was that the paper was really *good*...and it didn't mean a hill of beans to that teacher.

Like it or not, the farther along you are in school, the more likely you will suffer instructors enforcing their own idiosyncratic rules. My best advice is to heed Mark Twain: "Don't let school get in the way of your education."

Be proud of your work ... and show it

Do you know someone who counts every word of a 500-word assigned essay and rushes to conclude it as soon as he approaches that magic number?

How about the student who is convinced her chicken scratch is perfectly decipherable, even when the teacher has to wade through several cross-outs on every page and follow arrows from one page to another?

Or the one who spells a word correctly two or three times and incorrectly four or five others...all on the same page?

Teachers are human. They respond to presentation. If the *content* of two papers or projects is relatively equal, the *form* in which they're presented may well affect the grade, perhaps significantly.

There are a lot of teachers who make it a point to decrease grades because of poor grammar, spelling, or overall presentation, just as there are others who may award a better grade to a paper that was clearly prepared with care and pride.

Adapt to your teachers' quirks and foibles

Teachers differ in how they approach their subjects, as well as their expectations, standards, flexibility, and so on. It certainly is worth the effort to compile a "profile" of each of your teachers. What does each of them want to see in terms of notes, level of participation, papers, projects? What are their individual likes and dislikes? Their methods of grading and testing?

Knowing these various traits should certainly lead you to adapt your approach to each class. Let's say—not that it would ever happen to *you*, of course—that you have managed to dig yourself a very deep hole. It is 11 p.m., you're well past your study prime, and you still have reading assignments to complete for English and history tomorrow morning.

Your English teacher demands maximum class participation and makes it a large part of your grade—and test scores be damned. Her hobby seems to be calling on the unprepared, and she has an uncanny and unerring knack for ferreting out just those students.

Your history teacher discourages discussion and prefers to lecture and answer a couple of questions at the end of the class. He never calls on anyone for anything.

Given this situation, and knowing you can stay awake long enough to read only *one* of the two assignments, which would you choose?

Would there *ever* be a time, barring a simultaneous typhoon, eclipse, and national holiday, that you would show up for that English class unprepared?

While I'll show you in Chapter 5 how to ensure that poor scheduling does not become a habit that dooms you to such choices, I suspect far too many of you do not consider the natural differences among your teachers when scheduling homework, preparing papers, or studying for tests.

Likewise, I suspect far too few of you try to create a bond with one special teacher—a mentoring relationship—that could help you avoid some of the bumps and potholes along your route and make your journey far less troublesome. Why should you go out of your way to find a mentor? Because you probably need more help—in life, not just in school—than your friends or parents can provide. A mentor can give you that perspective, advice and help.

Let's get motivated!

Motivators are either intrinsic or extrinsic. What's the difference? You sign up for a voice class. Even if it were a subject necessary to fulfill an educational requirement, you chose it because you love singing.

You also signed up for biology. You hate the thought of dissecting frogs, and you couldn't care less whether they have exoskeletons, endoskeletons, or no skeletons at all, but the class is required.

In the first case, you're motivated by *intrinsic* factors—you are taking the voice class simply because you think you will enjoy it.

The second scenario is an example of *extrinsic* motivation. While you have no interest in biology, your reward for taking the class is external—you'll be able to graduate.

Extrinsic motivation can help you make it through boring or unpleasant tasks that are part of the process of reaching your goals. A vivid image of your final goal can be a powerful motivating force. One student dreamt of her future as a movie make-up artist whenever she needed a little motivation to get through an unrelated (and unwanted) class.

Try imagining a day in *your* life five or 10 years from now. If you can't, no *wonder* you're having a hard time motivating yourself.

A specific role model may also be an effective motivator. When she was a first grader, my daughter Lindsay became particularly enamored by Wilma Rudolph, who was born poor and black in the segregated South before World War II. Wilma contracted polio when she was four years old, had to wear a stiff leg brace for five years, and was told she would never walk normally again. My daughter thought it was amazing that Wilma, through sheer guts and determination, ultimately became the fastest woman in the world, winning four Olympic medals, three of them gold.

When confronted with her own (smaller!) problems, my 26-year-old daughter still reminds herself that "If Wilma could do it, I can, too." Think of your own role models in life. If you don't have any, find some!

Construct a goal pyramid

One way to easily visualize all your goals—and their relation to each other—is to construct a *goal pyramid*. Here's how to do it:

> ❯ Centered at the top of a piece of paper, write down what you hope to ultimately gain from your education. Where do you want to be and what do you hope to be doing three, five, or 10 years from now? This is your long-range goal and the pinnacle of your pyramid.
> ❯ Below your long-range goal(s), list mid-range goals, the milestones, or steps necessary to reach your eventual target.
> ❯ Below the mid-range goals, list as many short-range goals as you can—those incremental steps that can be completed in a relatively short period of time.

Update your goal pyramid as you progress through school. You may eventually decide on a different career. Or your mid-range goals may change as you choose a different path leading to the long-range goal. The short-range goals will undoubtedly change, sometimes daily.

The process of creating your own goal pyramid allows you to see *how* all those little daily and weekly steps you take can lead to your mid-range and long-term goals, which will motivate you to attack your daily and weekly tasks with more energy and enthusiasm.

How do you make setting goals a part of your life? Here are some hints I think will help:

> **Be realistic when you set goals.** Don't aim too high (or too low) and don't be particularly concerned when—not *if*—you have to make adjustments along the way.

> **Be realistic about your expectations.** Settle for a greater understanding of a subject for which you have little aptitude rather than futilely trying to master it.

> **Don't give up too easily.** You can be *overly* realistic—too ready to give up just because something is a trifle harder than you'd like. Don't aim too high and feel miserable when you don't come close, or aim too low and never achieve your potential—find the path that's right for you.

> **Concentrate on areas that offer the best chance for improvement.** Unexpected successes can do wonders for your confidence and might spur you to achieve more than you thought you could, even in other areas.

> **Monitor your achievements and keep reset-ting your goals.** Daily, weekly, monthly, yearly—ask yourself how you've done and where you'd like to go *now*.
> **Put your goal pyramid right up on the wall** or make it your computer's or phone's wallpaper. See it. Feel it. Live it every day.

Use rewards as artificial motivators

The way you decide to use a reward system depends on how much help you need getting motivated to study. Tasks that are intrinsically interesting require little outside motivation, but most schoolwork can be made more palatable by the promise of little rewards along the way. If the task is especially tedious or difficult, make the rewards more frequent so that your energy and determination don't flag.

The size of the reward should match the difficulty of the task. After an hour of reading, promise yourself a 15-minute snack break. After completing the rough draft of a long and complicated paper, treat yourself to a movie.

Four great ways to get super-organized

As you begin to make goal-setting and organization a part of your daily life, here are four concepts that will make a huge difference in your success.

Small changes can add up to big results

A simple, tiny change in your behavior may have virtually negligible results, but make *hundreds* of small changes, and the effects can be earth-shattering!

Make this rule become an automatic part of your thought process and your actions. It will help you understand the often small difference between success and failure, productivity and frustration, happiness and despair. Each change you make may seem inconsequential, but a host of small changes can lead to big successes.

The Pareto Principle

Victor Pareto was an Italian economist and sociologist at the turn of the 20th century who studied land ownership in Italy. Pareto discovered that more than 80 percent of all the land was owned by less than 20 percent of the people. As he studied other things that people owned (including money), he found the same principle held true: 20 percent or less of the people always ended up with 80 percent or more of whatever he measured.

The most interesting application of the 80-20 Rule is the corollary that relates directly to studying: If 20 percent of activities produce 80 percent of the results, then *80 percent of activities are only producing 20 percent of the results.*

To apply the Pareto Principle to managing *your* priorities, you should consistently ask yourself, "Which of my activities are part of the 20 percent?" In other words, which efforts are *not* contributing to the results you want to see?

Take advantage of "in-between" time

You can be even more productive if you learn to identify the little windows of opportunity that open each day. They don't arrive with much fanfare, so if you're not alert, you may not even notice them. What must you do with this "in-between" time when you are stuck in traffic, waiting in line, or on interminable hold? Recognize it as soon as it occurs and utilize it immediately by taking a premeditated action. If you don't have a plan, you will waste this time!

Here are some suggestions:

> Respond to emails or texts.
> Make a shopping list.
> Update or review your calendar or priority list.
> Clean your desk and return things to their proper places.
> Dejunk your inbox.
> Proofread some or all of one of your papers.
> Read a magazine or journal article.
> Read a newspaper.
> Think (about an upcoming assignment, a paper you're writing, any upcoming project).
> Relax!

I also strongly suggest you always carry a book you must (or want to) read...everywhere. You will often be able to finish entire chapters during otherwise wasted time. If you do a lot of driving, feel free to keep a couple of audiobooks handy, too.

Hide your phone!

If you are part of the generation that has grown up with laptops and tablets, smartphones and the Internet, you probably need little advice on how to efficiently use these tools in school (although I will give you some in future chapters).

But there is a dark side to the constant presence of cellphones and the concurrent and overwhelming growth of social media that I want to briefly address.

In less than a single decade, smartphones have taken over many people's lives. Their ubiquitous presence on buses and trains, in restaurants and movie theaters, and anyplace else that once promised to be an oasis of peace and quiet is, for many of us, a disturbing and annoying development.

But as intrusive as smartphones can be, it is the rise of social media and apps that have made them such a dangerous distraction for many students. I have little hope of changing my daughter's generational attraction to knowing what every one of her friends is thinking, doing, or thinking of doing *right now*. I am clearly not social enough to be a fan of social media.

There is a clear danger for students who, according to the *New York Times*, now spend, on average, three hours a day staring at their phones (which excludes any time actually *talking* on them). Couldn't we find better ways to spend *one eighth* of our time every day?

The habit of checking one's phone every few minutes just in case something has happened that you *must know right now* is clearly counterproductive to efficiently managing your time.

And it is virtually impossible to concentrate on *any* assignment when one's mobile device is pinging every time a text, email or app alert is received.

So please, feel free to use any or all of the fantastic technological tools now or soon to be available to help you study better and achieve better results.

But turn off, put down, and hide your cellphone while you study!

How perfect are you?

Superior students care about their work and consistently apply the effort necessary to achieve their goals.

Perfectionists care perhaps too much.

It is possible, of course, to score a "perfect" 100 on a test or to get an A+ on a paper the teacher calls "Perfect!" in the margin. But in reality, doing anything "perfectly" is an impossible task.

What does all this have to do with you? Nothing, unless you find yourself spending two hours polishing an already A+ paper or half an hour searching for that one "perfect" word or an hour rewriting great notes to make them "absolutely perfect." In other words, while striving for perfection may be a noble trait, it can very easily, perhaps inevitably, become an uncontrollable and unstoppable urge that negatively affects your work and your life.

If you find yourself fighting this demon, remind yourself (frequently) of the Law of Diminishing Returns: Your initial effort yields the biggest results, while each succeeding effort yields proportionately less. And there comes a point where even the most *prodigious* efforts yield *negligible* results. This applies not only to perfectionists, but also to those of you who scoff at the very thought of using a "simple" outline or producing a "formulaic" report. You do not have to always be innovative, dazzling, and creative. You do not have to invent a new, multimedia, interactive book report. It is not heretical to decide that a good, six-page, A- book report is acceptable, and that an A+ "innovation" is more trouble (and time!) than it's worth!

If you really would prefer spending another couple of hours polishing that A+ paper or recopying your perfectly good class notes for the third time instead of taking in a movie, reading a book for pleasure, or getting some *other* assignment done, be my guest. Is the extra effort *really* worth it? Maybe sometimes, but not usually.

Creating *your* study environment

On the following pages, I have included a checklist for you to analyze your study environment. It includes not just *where* you study but *when* and *how* you study, too. Once you've identified what works for you, avoid those situations in which you *know* you don't perform best. If you don't know the answer to one or more of the questions, take the time to experiment.

My Ideal Study Environment

How I receive information best:
1. ☐ Orally ☐ Visually

In the classroom, I should:
2. ☐ Concentrate on taking notes
   ☐ Concentrate on listening
3. ☐ Sit in front ☐ Sit in back ☐ Sit near a window or door

Where I study best:
4. ☐ At home ☐ In the library
   ☐ Somewhere else: _____

When I study best:
5. ☐ Every night; little on weekends ☐ Mainly on weekends
   ☐ Spread out over seven days
6. ☐ In the morning ☐ Evening ☐ Afternoon
7. ☐ Before dinner ☐ After dinner

How I study best:
8. ☐ Alone ☐ With a friend ☐ In a group
9. ☐ Under time pressure ☐ Before I know I have to
10. ☐ With music ☐ In front of the TV ☐ In a quiet room
11. ☐ Organizing an entire night's studying before I start
    ☐ Tackling and completing one subject at a time

I need to take a break:
12. ☐ Every 30 minutes or so ☐ Every hour ☐ Every 2 hours
    ☐ Every _____ hours

Many of the items on this chart should be understandable to you now. *Why* you feel the need for a particular environment is not important. Knowing you *have a preference* is. Here's what you're trying to assess in each item:

1. If you prefer "listening" to "seeing," you'll have little problem getting the information you need from class lectures and discussion. In fact, you'll *prefer* them to studying your textbooks. (You may have to concentrate on your reading skills and spend more time with your textbooks to offset this tendency. Highlighting or underlining your texts and/or taking detailed notes in the margins may help.)

If you're more of a "visual" person, you'll probably find it easier reading your textbook and may have to work to improve your classroom concentration. Taking excellent class notes that you can read later will probably be important for you. You'll also want to adapt your note-taking methods to your visual preference. Rather than writing notes like everybody else, draw pictures, use charts, or learn how to "map" a lecture.

2. This should tie in with your answer to (1). The more "aural" you are, the more you should concentrate on listening; the more "visual," the better your notes should be for later review.

3. This may make a difference for a number of reasons. You may find it difficult to hear or see from the back of the classroom. You may be shy and want to sit up front to motivate yourself to participate in class discussions or ask and answer questions in a lecture setting. You may find sitting near a window makes you feel a little less claustrophobic; alternatively, you may daydream too much if near a window and should sit as far "inside" the classroom as possible.

4. Whatever location you find most conducive to study (considering the limitations of your current living situation and schedule) should be where you spend most of your study time.

5. Deciding how to organize your time to most effectively cover the material may depend, in part, on the amount of homework you are burdened with and/or the time of year. You may have one schedule during most of the school year but have to adapt during test time, if papers are due, for special projects, and so on.

6. For some of you, such preferences may only be a factor on weekends, because your daytime hours are already scheduled—you're in middle or high school.

But if you're in college (or in a high school program that mimics college's "choose your own courses and times" scheduling procedures), you would want to use this factor in determining when to schedule your classes.

If you study best in the morning, for example, try to schedule as many classes as possible in the afternoons (or, at worst, late in the morning).

If you study best in the evening, either schedule morning classes and leave your afternoons free for other activities, or schedule them in the afternoons so you can sleep later (and study later the night before).

7. Some of us get cranky if we try to do *anything* when we're hungry. If you study poorly when your stomach is growling, eat something!

8. Most of us grow up automatically studying alone. If we study with a friend, there's often more talking, texting, TV watching...anything *but* studying. But don't underestimate the positive effect studying with one or two friends—or even a larger study group—can have on your schoolwork and grades. (I discuss study groups in greater detail at the end of this section.)

9. Just because you perform best under pressure doesn't mean you should always leave projects, papers, and studying for tests until the last minute. It just means you won't panic

(as much) when an unexpected project gets assigned or a surprise test is announced.

If you do *not* study well under pressure, it certainly doesn't mean you occasionally won't be required to do so. The better organized you are, the easier it will be for you to avoid panicking when the unexpected inevitably occurs.

10. Some of you (like me) will find it difficult to concentrate with*out* music or some sort of neutral background noise. Others couldn't sit in front of the TV or with cellphone in hand and study anything.

Many of you will fall in between—you can read and even take notes to music but need absolute quiet to study for a test or master particularly difficult concepts. If you don't know how you function best, now is the time to find out.

11. Choosing the second option—starting and finishing one project before moving on to another—doesn't mean you can't at least sit down and outline an entire night's study plan before tackling each subject in turn. Setting up such a study schedule *is* advised. But it may mean you really *can't* turn to another project while the first remains unfinished. Other people may have no problem working on one project, switching to another when they get stuck, then returning to the first.

12. There's nothing wrong with taking a break to keep yourself sharp and maximize your quality study time—as long as your breaks aren't every five minutes and they don't last longer than the study periods! In general, though, try to increase your concentration through practice so that you can go at least an hour before getting up. Too many projects will require at least that long to "get into" or organize, and you may find that breaking too frequently will require too much "review time" when you are ready to get back to work.

Study groups: What are friends for?

To form your own study group, identify a small group of like-minded students and share notes, question each other, and prepare for tests together. To be effective, obviously, the students you pick should share all, or at least most, of your classes.

Search out students who are smarter than you, but not too much smarter. If they are on a level far beyond your own, you'll soon be left in the dust and be more discouraged than ever. On the other hand, if you choose students who are too far beneath your level, you may enjoy being the smartest of the bunch but miss the point of the group: the challenge of other minds to spur you on.

Study groups can be organized in a variety of ways. Each member could be assigned primary responsibility for a single class, which would include preparing detailed notes from lectures and discussion groups. If supplementary reading is recommended but not required, that person could be responsible for doing all such reading and preparing detailed summaries.

Alternatively, each student can be responsible for his or her own notes, but the group could act as an *ad hoc* discussion group, refining understanding of key points, working on problems together, questioning each other, practicing for tests, and so forth.

Even if you find only one or two other students willing to work with you, such cooperation could be invaluable, especially in preparing for major exams.

How to form your own study group

> If possible, I suggest you invite a minimum of four students but no more than six. You want to ensure each student gets a chance to participate

as much as he or she wants, while maximizing the collective knowledge and wisdom of the group.

> While group members needn't be best friends, they shouldn't be overtly hostile to one another, either. Seek diversity of experience and demand common dedication.

> Try to select students who are at least as smart, committed, and serious as you. That will encourage you to keep up and challenge you a bit. Avoid a group in which you're the "star"—at least until you flicker out during the first exam.

> Avoid inviting members who are inherently unequal into the group—boyfriend/girlfriend combinations, in which one or the other may be inhibited by their *amore*'s presence; situations where one student works for another; situations where underclassmen and upperclassmen may stifle one another.

> Decide early on if you're forming a study group or a social group. If it's the latter, don't pretend it's the former. If the former, don't just invite your friends and informally sit around discussing your favorite podcasts for an hour each week.

> My personal preference is to assign each class to one student. That student must truly master that assigned class, completing any recommended additional reading, taking outstanding notes, outlining the course, being available for questions, and preparing various practice quizzes, midterms, and finals, as needed.

Needless to say, all of the other students still attend all classes, take their own notes, and do their own reading and homework assignments. But the student assigned a particular class should attempt to actually become the "substitute professor" of that class within the study group.

> Make meeting times and assignments formal and rigorous. Consider establishing rigid rules of conduct. Shake out the non-serious students early. You don't want anyone who is working as little as possible to take advantage of *your* hard work.

> Consider appointing a chair in charge of keeping everyone on schedule and settling disputes before they disrupt the group.

> However you organize your group, clearly decide—early—the exact requirements and assignments of each student. Again, you never want the feeling to emerge that one or two of you are trying to take advantage of the others.

Where should you study?

At any library. There may be numerous choices, from the large reading room to quieter, sometimes deserted specialty rooms to your own study cubicle. My favorite "home away from home" at college was a little room that seemingly only four or five of us knew about—with wonderfully comfortable chairs, subdued lighting, phonographs with earplugs, and a selection of some 500 classical records. For someone who likes to study to music, it was custom-made!

At home. Home is, of course, the most convenient place to make your study headquarters. It may not, however, be the most effective. It is unfortunately where distractions are most likely to occur. Little brothers (or your own kids) will not find you as easily in your library cubbyhole.

At a friend's, neighbor's, or relative's house. This may not be an option for most of you, even on an occasional basis, but you may want to set up one or two alternative study sites.

In an empty classroom. Certainly an option at many colleges and perhaps some private high schools, it is an interesting idea mainly because so few students have ever thought of it! While not a likely option at a public high school, it never hurts to ask if you can't make some arrangement. Since many athletic teams practice until 6 p.m. or later, even on the high school level, there may be a part of the school open—and usable with permission—even if the rest is locked up tight.

At your job. Whether you're a student working part-time or a full-timer going to school part-time, you may well be able to make arrangements to use an empty office, even during regular office hours, or perhaps after everyone has left (depending on how much your boss trusts you). If you're in middle or high school and a parent, friend, or relative works nearby, you may be able to study at his or her workplace.

Whatever place you choose for your study area, try to make it somewhere that is *only* for study. This eliminates your bed, in front of the TV, and the dining room table, among other bad choices.

If you associate your study area solely with homework—not sleeping, entertaining yourself, or eating—the time you spend will be more productive.

I would also recommend having a secondary study area available, for those times when your roommate (surprisingly) brings home a date or your primary study area is otherwise compromised.

When should you study

I recommend you create a routine time of day to study. Some experts contend that doing the same thing at the same time every day is the most effective way to organize any ongoing task. Some students find it easier to set aside specific blocks of time each day to study.

Whatever your own preference, the time of day you'll study most effectively is determined by these factors:

> *Study when you're at your best.* What is your peak performance period—the time of day you do your best work? This will vary from person to person—you may be dead to the world until noon but able to study well into the night, or up and alert at the crack of dawn but distracted and tired if you try to burn the midnight oil. Just remember: Focus = efficiency.

> *Consider your sleep habits.* Habit is a very powerful influence. If you always set your alarm for 7 a.m., you may soon start waking up moments before it rings. If you have grown accustomed to going to sleep around 11 p.m., you will struggle if you try to study until 2 a.m., and probably accomplish very little during those three hours.

> *Study when you can.* Although you should study when you are mentally most alert, external factors will play a role in deciding when you study. Being at your best is a great goal, but not always possible. Study whenever circumstances allow.

> *Consider the complexity of the assignment* when you allocate time. The tasks themselves may have a great effect on your schedule. If you are

a relatively slow reader, don't schedule half an hour to read a hundred pages of Tolstoy.

> *Use "nonprime" hours for the easiest tasks.* When you are least creative, least energetic, and least motivated, don't even think about tackling your most challenging assignments. Don't be like many businesspeople I know who schedule their time backwards: In the morning, when they're full of energy, they read the paper, check their email, and skim trade journals. At the *end* of the day, when they can barely see straight, they start on the presentation for the Board of Directors' meeting...*tomorrow's* Board of Directors' meeting.

> *Schedule study time immediately after class* or, if that's not possible, immediately before. This is most pertinent for college and graduate students, who may have significant free time between classes. Your memory of a class is, not surprisingly, strongest immediately afterward, so allocating an open hour after class to go over notes, revisit PowerPoint slides, and complete that day's assignment is the best way to spend that hour. Taking the time to study immediately *before* class is an excellent second option, especially if you usually need that time to complete that day's assignment.

Evaluate your study area

Whatever location you choose as your study base, how you set up your study area can affect your ability to stay focused and, if you aren't careful, seriously inhibit quality study time. Sit

down at your desk or study area right now and evaluate your
own study environment:

> Do you have one or two special places reserved
just for studying? Or do you study wherever
seems convenient or available at the time?

> Is your study area a pleasant place? Or do you
dread it because it's so depressing?

> How's the lighting? Is it too dim or too bright? Is
the entire area well-lit?

> Are all the materials you need handy?

> What else do you do here? Do you eat? Sleep?
Read for pleasure? If you try to study at the
same place you nap, you may find yourself doing
the latter when you are supposed to be doing
the former!

> Is your study area in a high-traffic area? How
often are you interrupted by people passing
through? Can you close the door to the room to
avoid disturbances and outside noise?

> When do you spend the most time here? What
time of day do you study? Is it when you are at
your best, or do you inevitably study when you're
tired and less productive?

> Are your files, folders, and other class materials
organized and near the work area? Do you have
an efficient filing system in place for them?

Staying focused on your studies

If you find yourself doodling and dawdling more than reading
and remembering, try these solutions:

❯ *Create a work environment in which you're comfortable.* The size, style, and placement of your desk, chair, and lighting may all affect whether or not you're distracted from the work at hand. Take the time to design the area that's perfect for you. Needless to say, anything that you know will distract you—a girlfriend's picture, a radio or TV, your cellphone—should disappear from your study area.

Remember: It is easier and more effective to simply remove a distraction, such as your cellphone, than to consciously try to avoid looking at it or responding to it.

❯ *Turn up the lights.* Experiment with the placement and intensity of lighting in your study area until you find what works for you, both in terms of comfort and as a means of staying awake and focused.

❯ *Set some rules.* Let family, relatives, and especially friends know how important your studying is and that specific hours are inviolate.

❯ *Take the breaks you need.* Don't just follow well-intentioned but bogus advice about how long you should study before taking a break. Break when *you* need to.

❯ *Select a study symbol.* Choose something you can associate with studying, such as a hat, a scarf, even one of those little trolls people keep on their desks. Whenever it's time to study, just jam on the hat, wrap yourself in the scarf, or set the troll prominently on your desk. It's study time! Not only will this "get you in the mood" to study, it will serve as a warning to room-mates, friends, or family members that you are working.

Don't associate your new "study symbol" with anything *but* studying. Don't wear your study hat to baseball games or leave your troll on the desk while you're on the phone with friends. The instant your study symbol is associated with something *other* than studying, it begins to lose its effectiveness as a study aid.

Fighting tiredness and boredom

"Man is the only animal that can be bored."
—ERICH FROMM

You've chosen the best study spot and no one could fault you on its setup. So why are you still falling asleep? Here's what to do if your energy and determination have gone on vacation together:

> ❯ *Take a nap.* Eureka: When you're too tired to study, take a short nap to revive yourself. Maximize that nap's effect by keeping it short—20 minutes is ideal, 40 minutes tops. After that, you go into another phase of sleep and you may wake more tired than before.
> ❯ *Have a drink.* A little caffeine won't harm you—a cup of coffee or tea, a glass of soda. Just be careful: Caffeine's "wake-up" properties seem to dissipate when you reach a certain level, making you far more tired than you were!
> ❯ *Turn down the heat.* You needn't build an igloo out back, but too warm a room will inevitably

leave you dreaming of sugarplums...while your paper remains unwritten on your desk.

> *Get some exercise.* Go for a walk, high step around the kitchen, do a few jumping jacks—even mild physical exertion will give you an immediate lift.

> *Change your study schedule.* Presuming you have some choice here, find a way to study when you are normally more awake and/or most efficient.

Studying with small kids

Since so many more of you are going to school while raising a family, I want to give you some ideas that will help you cope with the Charge of the Preschool Light Brigade:

> *Plan activities to keep the kids occupied.* The busier you are in school and/or at work, the more time your kids will want to spend with you when you *are* home. If you schedule *some* time with them, it may be easier for them to play alone the rest of the time, especially if you've created projects *they* can work on while *you're* working on your homework.

> *Make them part of your study routine.* Kids love routine, so why not include them in yours? If 4 p.m. to 6 p.m. is always "Mommy's Study Time," they will soon get used to it, especially if you make spending other time with them a priority and dream up some fun things for them to do during those hours. Explaining the importance of what you're doing—in a way that includes some ultimate benefit for *them*—will also motivate them to be part of your "study team."

> *Use the television as a babysitter.* While many of you will have a problem with this—it's one that I and my daughter dealt with daily, if not hourly—it may be the lesser of two evils. And you can certainly rent (or DVR or TiVo or download) enough quality shows to avoid sexual or violent content.

> *Plan your study accordingly.* All these suggestions will not keep your kids from interrupting every now and then. While you can minimize such intrusions, you will never eliminate them entirely. So don't try—plan your schedule *assuming* them. For one, that means taking more frequent breaks to spend five minutes with your kids. They'll be more likely to give you the time you need if they get periodic attention themselves.

> *Find help.* Spouses can occasionally take the kids out for dinner and a movie. (Trust me, the kids will encourage you to study *more* if you institute this practice.) Relatives can babysit (at their homes) on a rotating basis. Playmates can be invited over (allowing you to send your darling to their house the next day). You may be able to trade babysitting dates with other parents at school. And professional daycare may be available at your child's school or in someone's home for a couple of hours a day.

What is *your* special talent?

It is the rare individual who is superior, or even good, in *every* subject. Most of us are a little better in one subject or another.

Some of us simply *like* one subject more than another—and don't think *that* doesn't change your attitude toward it. Others are naturally gifted in one area, average in others.

For example, skill with numbers and spatial relations may come easily to you, but you may have absolutely no ear for music or languages. Or you may find learning a language to be a piece of cake, but not have the faintest clue why Pythagoras came up with his Theorem or why you should care. Some students are good with their hands. Others may find making the simplest item torturous, and the results embarrassing.

My advice is to shift some study time from those tasks easily achieved to those that you find more difficult. The balance you will see in your development will be worth the effort.

And if you've never really thought about the subjects you like and dislike, use the chart at the end of this chapter to identify them. You'll also be asked to identify those in which you perform well or poorly. (Your report card will confirm those!) Use this list to organize your own schedule so you can take advantage of your natural talents and devote additional time to the subject areas that need the most work.

And if you have a choice

All college students—and some high school students—are able to pick and choose courses according to their own schedules, likes, dislikes, goals, and so on. The headiness of such freedom should be tempered with the commonsense approach you're trying to develop by reading this book. Here are a few hints to help you along:

> ❯ Whenever possible, *consider each professor's reputation* as you decide whether to select a particular course (especially if it is an overview

or introductory course offered in two or more sections). Word soon gets around as to which professors' lectures are stimulating and rewarding and whose are a cure for insomnia.

> Attempt to *select classes that balance your schedule* on a weekly, even daily, basis, though that will not always be possible or advisable. (Don't change your major just to suit your schedule!) Try to leave an open hour or half-hour between classes—it's ideal for review, post-class note-taking, quick trips to the library or online, and so on.

> *If there is a course you'd like to take* but can't fit into this semester's schedule, consider attending the first class, which is generally an overview of the entire course. You will be able to pick up a syllabus and get a feel for the professor's style.

> Try to *alternate challenging classes with those that come more easily* to you. Studying is a process of positive reinforcement. You'll need encouragement along the way.

> *Avoid late-evening or early-morning classes*, especially if such scheduling provides you with large gaps of "down time."

> *Set a personal study pace and follow it.* Place yourself on a study diet, the key rule of which is: *Don't overeat.*

The landscape is littered with the shadows of unsuccessful students who have failed in their pursuits—*not* because they lacked talent or motivation, but because they succumbed to information overload and pressure.

You *can* be successful without killing yourself!

Evaluation of Subject Areas

List the subject areas/courses you like most:

_____

_____

_____

_____

_____

List those you like least:

_____

_____

_____

_____

_____

List the courses in which you get the best grades:

_____

_____

_____

_____

_____

And those in which you get the worst grades:

_____

_____

_____

_____

_____

Chapter 3

Read with Purpose

"Some books are to be tasted, others to be swallowed, and some few to be chewed and digested."

—Francis Bacon

I am a reader. But the fact that I have always loved to read didn't make it any easier to face some of those deadly textbook reading assignments in high school or college. As a student, you inevitably will be required to spend hours poring through ponderous, convoluted reading assignments for subjects that are required but not exactly scintillating.

You may love reading novels, short stories, or poetry but have trouble with textbook assignments for certain subjects. You may finish reading a long passage and forget it almost immediately. Or you just may hate the thought of sitting still to read *anything*. Whatever kind of student you are—and whatever your level of reading skill—this chapter will help you surmount your reading challenge

You will learn what you should read and what you don't have to. You'll discover how to reduce the time you spend reading, how to identify the main ideas and important details, and how to remember more of what you read.

Of Kindles, Kobos, and Nooks

The original E-readers—Kindle, Kobo, Nook, and others—enabled you to read a digital edition of a book...and little else. The most current E-readers are actually tablet computers that include the pertinent digital architecture within them, allowing you to use features that may include a touchscreen, stylus, attachable keyboard, and so forth. As a result, you can now take notes, underline, highlight, color code, and otherwise mark up a digital edition.

If you already prefer a digital book to a printed copy, even if your normal slate consists exclusively of romance, sci-fi, and/or graphic novels, you will probably have no problem reading more serious literature on your tablet.

While many (but certainly not all) textbooks, magazines, journals, and newspapers are now also available digitally, you may find their digital editions cumbersome or just not as easy to use.

As long as you apply the advice in this chapter to your reading assignments, you may choose whichever format you prefer—print, digital or, for that matter, audio.

Define your purpose for reading

What is your purpose for reading? Reading a chapter just so you can proclaim, "Okay, I finished *that* assignment" is relatively futile. You may as well tuck the book under your pillow and hope to absorb it by osmosis while you sleep.

There are six fundamental purposes for reading:

1. To grasp a certain message
2. To find important details
3. To answer a specific question
4. To evaluate what you are reading
5. To apply what you are reading
6. To be entertained

Use the clues in your textbooks

There are special sections found in nearly all textbooks and technical materials (in fact, in almost all books except novels) that contain a wealth of information and can help you glean more from your reading. Becoming familiar with this data will enrich your reading experience and often make it easier. Here's what to look for:

The first page after the title page is usually the *table of contents*—a chapter-by-chapter list of the book's contents. Some are surprisingly detailed, listing every major point or topic covered in each chapter.

The first prose section (after the title page, table of contents, and, perhaps, acknowledgments page) is the *preface,* usually a description of the information you will find in the book. Authors may also use the preface to point out unique aspects of their books.

The *introduction* may be in place of or in addition to the preface and be written by the author or some "name" the author has recruited to lend additional prestige to his or her work. Most introductions are an even more detailed overview of the book—chapter-by-chapter summaries are often included to give the reader a feel for the material to be covered.

Footnotes may be found throughout the text (a slightly elevated number following a sentence or quote: "jim dandy"[24]) and either explained at the bottom of the page on which they appear or as endnotes in a special section at the back of the chapter or book. Footnotes may be used to cite sources of direct quotes or ideas, to further explain a point, or to add information outside of the text. You may learn to make it a habit to ferret out sources cited in this way for further reading.

If a text tends to use an alarming number of unfamiliar terms, a considerate author will include a *glossary*—essentially an abridged dictionary that defines all such terms.

The *bibliography*, usually at the end of the book, may include the source material the author used to research the textbook, a list of "recommended reading," or both. It is usually organized alphabetically by subject, making it easy for you to find more information on a specific topic.

Appendices containing supplementary data or examples relating to subject matter covered in the text may also appear in the back of the book.

The last thing in a book is usually the *index*, an alphabetical listing that references, by page number, every mention of a particular name, subject, and topic in the text.

Making it a habit to utilize all of these tools provided in most textbooks can only make your studying easier.

Find other textbooks if necessary

Although the authors and editors of many textbooks might be experts in their subjects, even legends in their fields, writing in jargon-free, easy-to-grasp prose is probably not their strong suit. You will occasionally be assigned a textbook that is so obtuse you aren't sure whether to read it front to back, upside down, or inside out.

If you find a particular chapter, section, or entire textbook impossible to understand, find *another* book covering the *same* subject area that you *can* understand. You may even ask your teacher for a recommendation, which may make your search for a *readable* text much easier. Just don't ask her why she selected that torturous text in the first place.

If you just don't get it, maybe it's because the *author* just doesn't know how to *explain* it. *Maybe it's not your fault!* Too many students have sweated, moaned, dropped classes, even changed majors because they thought they were dumb, when it's possible it's the darned textbook that's dense, not you.

I realize this may be more work than you bargained for (or you think I promised), but wasting hours trying to make sense of ponderous prose could easily waste even more time.

If another book finally helps you understand the subject, the original textbook may be easier to fathom...presuming you need it at all.

Use the clues in each chapter

Begin with a very quick overview of the assignment, looking for questions that you'd like answered. Consider the following elements of your reading assignment *before* you begin your reading:

Chapter titles and boldfaced heads and subheads announce the detail about the main topic. And, in some textbooks, paragraph headings or boldfaced "lead-ins" announce that the author is about to provide finer details.

So start each reading assignment by going through the chapter, beginning to end, *reading only the boldfaced heads and subheads.*

Look for end-of-chapter summaries. Knowing what the author deems important will help you look for the building blocks of his conclusions while you're reading.

Most textbooks, particularly those in the sciences, will have charts, graphs, numerical tables, maps, and other illustrations. Be sure to observe how they supplement the text and what points they emphasize, and make note of these.

In some textbooks, you'll discover that key terms and information are highlighted within the body text. To find the definitions of these terms may then be your purpose for reading.

Some textbook publishers use a format in which key points are emphasized by questions, either within the body of or at the end of the chapter. If you read these questions *before* reading the chapter, you'll have a better idea of what material you need to pay closer attention to.

Three ways to read

Depending on what you're trying to accomplish in a particular reading assignment and the kind of book involved, there are three different ways to read. Knowing when to use each will make any assignment easier:

1. **Quick reference reading** seeks specific information that addresses a particular question or concern the reader has.
2. **Critical reading** is used to discern ideas and concepts that require a thorough analysis.
3. **Aesthetic or pleasure reading** is for sheer entertainment or to appreciate an author's style and ability.

The importance of pre-reading

The best way to begin any reading assignment is to skim the pages to get an overview of what information is included, seeking some of the "clues" we've previously discussed. Then read the text carefully, word-for-word, and highlight, underline, or take notes in your notebook, on your computer, or in the book itself.

A brief digression: Most everyone I know confuses the words "skim" and "scan." Let me set the record straight.

Skim is to read quickly and superficially.

Scan is to read carefully but for a specific item.

So when you *skim* a reading selection, you are reading it in its entirety, though you're only hitting the "highlights." When you *scan* a selection, you are reading it in detail but only until you find what you're looking for. Scanning is the *fastest* reading rate of all—although you are reading in detail, you are *not* seeking to comprehend or remember anything that you see *until you find the specific information you're looking for.*

You probably are assigned a lot of reading that can be accomplished by skimming for facts. By establishing the questions you want answered *before* you begin to read, you can quickly go through the material, extracting only the information you need.

Let's say you're reading a science book with the goal of identifying the function of a cell's nucleus. You can breeze through the section that describes the parts of the cell and skim the description of what cells do. You already know what you're looking for—and there it is in the section that talks about what each cell part does. Now you can start to *read*.

By identifying the questions you wanted to answer (*a.k.a.* your purpose) in advance, you would be able to skim the chapter and answer your questions in a lot less time than it would have taken to painstakingly read every word.

Skimming, or pre-reading, is a valuable step even if you aren't seeking specific facts. When skimming for a general overview, there's a very simple procedure to follow:

> If there is a title or heading, *rephrase it as a question*. This will be your purpose for reading.

> Examine all the *subheadings, illustrations, and graphics*, as these will help you identify the significant matter within the text.

> Read thoroughly the *introductory paragraphs*, the summary, and any questions at the chapter's end.

> Read the *first sentence* of every paragraph, which generally contains the main point of the paragraph.

> *Evaluate* what you have gained from this process: Can you answer the questions at the end of the chapter? Could you intelligently participate in a class discussion of the material?

> *Write* a brief summary that encapsulates what you have learned from your skimming.

> Based on your evaluation, *decide* whether a more thorough reading is required.

As a general rule, if you are reading textbook material word for word, you probably are wasting quite a bit of your study time. Good readers are able to discern what they should read in this manner and what they can afford to skim.

When trying to simply gather detail and facts, skimming a text is a simple and very important shortcut that can save you a lot of reading time. Even if a more in-depth reading is necessary, you will find that by having gone through this process, you will have developed the kind of skeletal framework that will make your further reading faster, easier, and more meaningful.

Whether you're skimming or scanning, you will have equipped yourself with the ability to better digest whatever the author is trying to communicate.

Words may also be clues

While the heads, subheads, first sentences, and other author-provided hints will help you get a quick read on what a chapter's about, some of the *words* in that chapter will help you home in on the important points and ignore the unimportant. Knowing when to speed up, slow down, stop, or really concentrate will help you read both faster *and* more effectively.

When you see words such as "likewise," "in addition," "moreover," "furthermore," and the like, you should know nothing new is being introduced. If you already know what's going on, you can speed up or skip what's coming entirely.

On the other hand, when you see words like "on the other hand," "nevertheless," "however," "rather," "but," and their ilk, slow down—you're getting information that adds a new perspective or contradicts what you've just read.

Lastly, watch out for "payoff" words such as, "in conclusion," "therefore," "thus," "consequently," and "to summarize," especially if you only have time to "hit the high points" of a chapter or if you're reviewing for a test. Here's where the author has tied up everything that came before in a nice bow. This unexpected present may help you avoid having to unwrap the entire chapter.

Now go back for detail

If a more thorough reading of a text is required, go back to the beginning. *Read one section (chapter, unit, whatever) at a time.*

As you read, make sure you know what's going on by asking yourself if the passage is written to address one of these five questions:

1. **Who?** The paragraph focuses on a particular person or group of people. The topic sentence tells you *who* this is.

2. **When?** The paragraph is primarily concerned with *time*. The topic sentence may even begin with the word "when."

3. **Where?** The paragraph is oriented around a particular place or location. The topic sentence states *where* you are reading about.

4. **Why?** A paragraph that states reasons for some belief or happening usually addresses this question. The topic sentence answers *why* something is true or *why* an event happened.

5. **How?** The paragraph identifies the way something works or the means by which something is done. The topic sentence explains the *how* of what is described.

Do not go on to the next chapter or section until you've completed the following exercise:

> Write definitions of any key terms you feel are essential to understanding the topic.

> Write questions and answers you feel clarify the topic.

> Write any questions for which you *don't* have answers—then make sure you find them through rereading, further research, or asking another student or your teacher.

> ❯ Even if you still have unanswered questions, move on to the next section and complete numbers one to three for that section (and so on, until your reading assignment is complete).

The challenge of technical texts

You've already learned a lot of ways to improve your reading. It's time to examine the unique challenges posed by highly technical texts—physics, trigonometry, chemistry, calculus— you know, subjects that three-fourths of all students avoid like the plague. More than any other kind of reading, these subjects demand a logical, organized approach, a step-by-step reading method. And they require detecting and understanding the text's *organizational devices.*

Developing the skill to identify the basic sequence of the text will enable you to follow the progression of thought, a progression that is vital to your comprehension and retention.

Why? In most technical writing, each concept is like a building block of understanding—if you don't understand a particular section or concept, you won't be able to understand the *next* section, either.

Most technical books are saturated with ideas, terms, formulas, and theories. The chapters are dense with information, compressing a great wealth of ideas into a few pages. They demand to be read very carefully.

In order to get as much as possible from such reading assignments, you can take advantage of some devices to make sense of the organization. Here are five basics to watch for:

1. Definitions and terms
2. Examples

3. Classifications and listings
4. Use of contrast
5. Cause-effect relationships

In reading any specialized text, you must begin at the beginning—understanding the jargon particular to that discipline. Everyday words can have a variety of meanings, some of them even contradictory, depending on the context in which they're used. These same familiar words may have very precise definitions in technical writing.

For example, the definition of elasticity (*the ability of a solid to regain its shape after a deforming force has been applied*) is the same in Las Vegas or Las Palmas. Such exact terminology enables scientists to communicate with the precision their discipline requires.

Definitions may vary in length. One term may require a one-sentence definition, others entire paragraphs, and some a whole chapter to accurately communicate their meanings.

Look for key words that indicate specific mathematical operations. You need to *add* when you see words such as "increased by," "combined," "together," "sum," or "total of "; *subtract* when you see "decreased by," "minus," "less," "difference"; *multiply* when you see "product," "increased," "by a factor of," and "times"; and *divide* when you see "per," "ratio," "quotient," or "percent."

Another communication tool is the example. Technical writing often is filled with new or foreign ideas—many of which are not readily digestible. They are difficult in part because they are abstract. Authors use examples to construct a bridge from abstract principles to concrete illustrations. These examples are essential to your ability to comprehend intricate and complicated theories.

Unlike other writing, technical writing places a very high premium on brevity in order to compress a great deal of knowledge into a relatively small space. Few technical texts or articles include anecdotal matter or chatty stories about the author's experiences.

A third tool frequently utilized in texts is classification and listings. Classifying is the process by which common subjects are categorized under a general heading. Especially in technical writing, authors use classification to categorize extensive lists of detail.

A fourth tool used in communicating difficult information is that of comparing and contrasting. Texts use this tool to bring complicated material into focus by offering a similar or opposing picture. Through comparison, a text relates a concept to one that has been previously defined—or to one a reader may readily understand. Through contrast, the text concentrates on the differences and distinctions between two ideas.

A final tool that texts employ to communicate is the cause-effect relationship, the fundamental quest of most scientific research. Science begins with the observation of the effect—what is happening? It is snowing. The next step is to conduct research into the cause: *Why* is it snowing? Detailing this cause-effect relationship is often the essence of scientific and technical writing.

Cause-effect relationships may be written in many ways. The effect may be stated first, followed by the cause. An effect may be the result of several connected causes—a causal chain. And a cause may have numerous effects.

Read with a plan

More than any other type of writing, highly specialized technical writing must be read with a plan. You can't approach your reading assignment merely with the goal of completing it. Such mindless reading will leave you confused and frustrated, drowning in an ocean of theories, concepts, terms, and examples.

Your plan should incorporate the following guidelines:

> *Learn the terms* that are essential to understanding the concepts presented. Knowing the precise definitions an author uses will enable you to follow his chain of thought from page to page and chapter to chapter.

> *Determine the structure* or organization of the text. Most chapters have a pattern that forms the skeleton for the material. A book may begin with a statement of a theory, give examples, provide sample problems, and then summarize. Often this pattern can be discerned through a preview of the table of contents or the titles and subtitles.

> *Skim the chapter* to get a sense of the author's viewpoint. Ask questions to define your purpose for reading. Use any summaries or review questions to guide your approach.

> Do a thorough *analytical reading* of the text. Do not proceed from one section to the next until you have a clear understanding of the section you are reading—the concepts generally build upon each other.

> *Review immediately* upon concluding your thorough reading. Write a summary of the concepts and theories you need to remember. Answer any questions raised when you skimmed the text. Do the problems and, if possible, apply the formulas.

Technical material is saturated with ideas. You will want to read such material with the utmost concentration—it is not meant to be sped through.

Good readers know that such material demands reading slowly in order to achieve the greatest level of retention: Every definition has to be digested, every formula understood, every example considered.

If you're having difficulty reading such texts—or attempting to work out technical problems—try the following "tricks":

> Whenever you can, "translate" formulas and numbers into words. To test your understanding, try to put your translation into *different* words.

> Pictures may help, even if you aren't a particularly visual learner. Try turning a particularly vexing math problem into a drawing or diagram.

> Before you even get down to solving a problem, try to estimate the answer. This is an easy way to make sure you wind up in the right ballpark.

> Play around. There are often different paths to the same solution, or even equally valid solutions. If you find one, try to find others.

> When you are checking your calculations, try working *backward*. It is an easy way to catch simple mathematical errors.

> Try to figure out what is being asked, what principles are involved, what information is important, and what's not.

> Teach someone else. Trying to explain mathematical or scientific concepts to someone will quickly pinpoint what you really know or don't know.

> For long lists of items you simply must memorize—all the bones of the human body, a series of chemical formulas, basic scientific definitions—consider preparing flashcards. While an "old school" method, they may be an effective way for some of you to remember such items (and, for that matter, obscure vocabulary words or translations of foreign words and phrases). I'll discuss other memory techniques in the next chapter.

Aesthetic (pleasure) reading

"A great book should leave you with many experiences, and slightly exhausted at the end. You live several lives while reading it."

—WILLIAM STYRON

Most fiction is an attempt to tell a story. There is a beginning, in which characters and setting are introduced. There is a conflict or struggle that advances the story to a climax—where the conflict is resolved. A final *denouement* or "winding up" concludes the story. Your literature class will address these parts using terms that are often more confusing than helpful. The following are brief definitions of some of the more important ones:

Plot: The order or sequence of the story—how it proceeds from opening through climax. Your ability to understand and appreciate literature depends upon how well you follow the plot—the *story*.

Characterization: The personalities or characters central to the story—the heroes, heroines, villains, and supporting characters. You will want to identify the main characters of the story and understand how they relate to the struggle and each other.

Theme: The controlling message or subject of the story; the moral or idea that the author is using the plot and characters to communicate.

Setting: The time and place in which the story occurs. This is especially important when reading a historical novel or one set in another culture.

Point of view: Who is telling the story? Is it one of the central characters giving you flashbacks? Or is it a third-person narrator offering commentary and observations on the characters, the setting, and the plot?

The first step is to familiarize yourself with these concepts, then try to recognize them in each novel or short story you read. As you begin your reading, approach it from an aesthetic standpoint: How does it make you feel? What do you think of the characters? Do you like them? Hate them? Relate to them?

Second, make sure you know what's going on—this involves the plot and the development of the characters. On a chapter-by-chapter basis, you may find it helpful to keep a sheet of paper on which you can write a sentence or two of the plot development and note any new characters introduced.

How fast can you understand?

"When we read too fast or too slowly, we understand nothing."

—BLAISE PASCAL

Are you worried that you read too slowly? You probably shouldn't be—less-rapid readers are not necessarily less able. What counts is what you comprehend and remember. And like anything else, practice will probably increase your reading speed.

If you demand a ranking, read the 300-word selection below (from *Awaken Your Third Eye* by Susan Shumsky) from start to finish, noting the elapsed time on your watch. Score yourself as follows:

Under 30 seconds	very fast
31–45 seconds	fast
46–60 seconds	high average
61–89 seconds	average
90–119 seconds	slow
120 seconds or more	very slow

In Homer's Odyssey, composed in the 8th century BC, we find an allegory about the third eye. After the Trojan War, the hero Odysseus is traveling home to Ithaca. He lands on Sicily, home of the Cyclopes, where he encounters a cruel, savage giant, Polyphemus (son of Poseidon) with a large eye in the middle of his forehead. Odysseus and his sailors are imprisoned in a cave by the giant, who makes meals of six of them. Odysseus tricks the giant into getting drunk. In his weakened and vulnerable state, Polyphemus falls asleep and Odysseus drives a firebrand into his eye, blinding him. Odysseus and his remaining band barely escape the island with their lives.

In India, the word *chakra* literally means "wheel." The third eye chakra is found in the middle of the forehead, where the Cyclopes eye is located. Remarkably, the Greek work Cyclopes means "wheel-eyed."

With that in mind, we might consider the possible interpretations of the Polyphemus myth. One explanation is that piercing the eye of Polyphemus represents atrophy of the third eye and subsequent loss of divine wisdom. Another might be that if the spiritual gifts granted through opening the third eye are misused, one is vulnerable to destruction.

The ancient Greeks believed the pineal gland to be the entrance to the realms of thought. Plato (circa 428 BC–348 BC) and Hippocrates (circa 460 BC–377 BC) believed the third eye (enkephalos) to be the "eye of wisdom." Plato viewed the chakras as subtle organs through which the soul (psyche) communicates with the physical body. He thought the marrow or cerebrospinal fluid to be the essence of the soul, and that the chakras emanated spiritual energy by means of this spiritual sap, which he called "radical moisture." He saw the third eye as the controlling center for all the chakras.

A good reader should have tested fast or very fast and be able to easily summarize the selection's main points.

What decreases speed/comprehension?

> Reading aloud or moving your lips when you read.
> Reading mechanically—using your finger to follow words and moving your head along as you read.
> Applying the wrong *kind* of reading to the material.
> Lacking sufficient vocabulary.

To increase your reading speed

> Focus your attention and concentration.
> Eliminate outside distractions.

> Read in an uncluttered, comfortable environment.

> Don't get hung up on single words or sentences, but *do* look up (in the dictionary) key words that you must understand in order to grasp an entire concept.

> Try to grasp overall concepts rather than attempting to understand every detail.

> If you find yourself moving your lips when you read (vocalization), practice reading with a pen or some other (nontoxic, non-sugary) object in your mouth. If it falls out while you're reading, you know you have to keep working!

> Build your vocabulary. You may be reading slowly (and/or having trouble understand-ing what you read) because your vocabulary is insufficient for your reading level.

> Read more...and more often. Reading is a habit that improves with practice.

> Avoid rereading words or phrases. According to one study, an average student reading at 250 words per minute rereads 20 times per page. The slowest readers reread the most.

To increase your comprehension

> Try to make the act of learning sequential—comprehension is built by adding new knowl-edge to existing knowledge.

> Review and rethink at designated points in your reading. Test yourself to see if the importance of the material is getting through.

> If things don't add up, discard your conclusions. Go back, reread, and try to find an alternate conclusion.

> Summarize what you've read, rephrasing it in your notes in your own words.

Most importantly, read at the speed that's comfortable for you. Though I *can* read extremely fast, I *choose* to read literature much more slowly so I can appreciate an author's word play. Likewise, any material that I find particularly difficult to grasp slows me right down. I read newspapers, popular magazines, and the like very fast, seeking to grasp the important information but not every detail.

Should you take some sort of speed reading course, especially if your current speed level is low?

Reading for speed has some merit—many people who are slow readers read as little as possible, simply because they find it so tedious and boring. But just reading faster is not the answer to becoming a good reader.

While I doubt such a course could hurt, if you just keep practicing reading, you will increase your speed naturally.

Remember more of what you read

I will show you additional techniques to remember more of what you read in the next chapter, but here are some general suggestions you will find helpful.

Each time you attempt to read something that you must recall, use this six-step process to assure you'll remember:

1. **Evaluate the material.** Define your purpose for reading. Identify your interest level and get a sense of how difficult the material is.

2. **Choose appropriate reading techniques** for the purpose of your reading.

3. **Identify the important facts** and remember what you need to. Let your purpose for reading dictate what you remember, and identify associations that connect the details to recall.

4. **Take notes.** Use your own words to write a synopsis of the main ideas. Use an outline, diagram, or concept tree to show relationship and patterns. Writing down key points will further reinforce your ability to remember.

5. **Review.** Quiz yourself on those things you *must* remember. Develop some system by which you review your notes at least three times before you are required to recall the material. The first review should be shortly after you have read the material, the second a few days later, and the final review just before you are expected to recall. This process will help you avoid cram sessions.

6. **Implement.** Find opportunities to *use* the knowledge you have gained. Study groups and class discussions are invaluable opportunities to put what you have learned to good use. Participating in group discussions will greatly increase what you recall.

Highlight or underline

Highlighting or underlining key words and phrases in your textbook may be an effective way for some of you to remember more and streamline your review process. Just be selective— if you find that rereading your highlighted sections is nearly equivalent to reading the whole textbook again, you are highlighting too much!

I developed a set of rules for making the most of my highlighters during college as my workload became much heavier:

> I highlighted areas of the text with which I didn't feel completely comfortable.
> I identified single words and sentences that encapsulated a section's major ideas or themes.
> I concentrated on the key words, facts, and concepts, and skipped the digressions, multiple examples, and unnecessary explanations.
> I underlined or highlighted my classroom notes as well as texts to make studying from them easier.

To sharpen your underlining and highlighting skills, read through the three paragraphs on page 93 (excerpted from *Compassionate Capitalism* by Marc Benioff and Karen Southwick) and identify the key sentence(s) or words.

Take Notes

Alternatively, you can take notes in the margins of your textbook. This may make it easier for you to rank the facts conveyed by the text.

I used to use a little shorthand method to help me remember written materials. I'd draw vertical lines close to the text to assign levels of importance. One vertical line meant that the material should be reviewed; two indicated that the facts were very important; asterisks signified "learn or fail" material. I'd insert question marks for material that I wanted one of my more intelligent friends or a teacher to explain to me further. I'd use circles to indicate the information I was dead sure would show up on the next test.

I found that the very act of assigning relative weights of importance to the text and keeping a lookout for test material sharpened my attention and helped me remember more.

Become an active reader

I urge you to quiz yourself on written material to ascertain how well you retain it. If this doesn't work, try asking the questions *before* you read the material.

For instance, even though I have been an avid reader throughout much of my academic life, I had some trouble with the reading comprehension sections of standardized tests the first couple of times I attempted them. Why? I think I had a tendency to rush through these sections.

Then someone suggested to me that I read the questions *before* I read the passage. Presto! Great scores in reading comp (765 points on my verbal SAT for all of you doubters!).

While you won't always have such a ready-made list of questions, there are other sources: the summaries at the beginnings of chapters and the synopses in tables of contents. Pay attention to these.

Organize the material

Our minds crave order. Optical illusions work because the mind is bent on imposing order on every piece of information perceived by the senses. As you read, think of ways to organize the material to help your mind absorb it.

I always liked diagrams with single words and short phrases connected with arrows to show cause and effect relationships. Or I would highlight in texts the *reasons* things occurred with a special mark (I used a triangle).

Develop good reading habits

It's impossible for anyone to remember what he read at 3 a.m., or while waiting to go on the biggest date of his life. Are you a morning person? Then wake up early to do your reading. Do you not get going until after lunch? Then get your reading done before dinner.

At most companies, corporate philanthropy typically gets started in one of two ways. The first way occurs when the CEO gets very passionate about a particular cause and decides to donate personal and/or corporate money to it. The second way is when the company decides that it needs to do philanthropy for PR/marketing reasons and begins making grants, either through a corporate giving program or a foundation.

There are obvious flaws with both of these approaches. In the first, philanthropy never really becomes part of the culture, but is dependent upon the CEO's whim and can be turned off or on depending on his or her devotion to the cause. Even though passionate CEOs can do great things in charitable giving, there's a risk that the commitment may not survive the CEO's time at the top, especially in these days of rampant CEO turnover. Not only that, the CEO's passion may not fit well with the company's business, which again can cause philanthropy to sputter out if the CEO leaves or gets diverted by other issues.

In the second scenario, the company proclaims that it has, say, $500,000 or $1 million to give away, and is immediately inundated by requests from all sides. Every group, from schools to homeless shelters to outdoor theater companies to struggling artists, seeks a share of the largesse. The corporate philanthropy is largely reactive, responding to grant proposals, rather than proactive, putting in place a program that makes sense for the company and spelling out the types of projects it will consider. The motivation—to gain PR plaudits—is viewed as cynical by employees, so it does not engage them. Ultimately, the commitment is superficial and easily dislodged in difficult times.

Which words or phrases did you underline in this example on page 93? Here is what I did:

At most companies, corporate philanthropy typically gets started in one of two ways. The first way occurs ① when the CEO gets very passionate about a particular cause and decides to donate personal and/or corporate money to it. The second way is ② when the company decides that it needs to do philanthropy for PR/marketing reasons and begins making grants, either through a corporate giving program or a foundation.

There are obvious flaws with both of these approaches. In the first, ① philanthropy never really becomes part of the culture, but is dependent upon the CEO's whim and can be turned off or on depending on his or her devotion to the cause. Even though passionate CEOs can do great things in charitable giving, there's a risk that the commitment may not survive the CEO's time at the top, especially in these days of rampant CEO turnover. Not only that, the CEO's passion may not fit well with the company's business, which again can cause philanthropy to sputter out if the CEO leaves or gets diverted by other issues.

In the second scenario, the company proclaims that it has, say, $500,000 or $1 million to give away, and is immediately ② inundated by requests from all sides. Every group, from schools to homeless shelters to outdoor theater companies to struggling artists, seeks a share of the largesse. The corporate philanthropy is largely reactive, responding to grant proposals, rather than proactive, putting in place a program that makes sense for the company and spelling out the types of projects it will consider. The motivation—to gain PR plaudits—is viewed as cynical by employees, so it does not engage them. Ultimately, the commitment is superficial and easily dislodged in difficult times.

Build your own library

"Some books are undeservedly forgotten; none are undeservedly remembered."

—W.H. AUDEN

If you are ever to become an active, avid reader, access to books will do much to cultivate the habit. I suggest you "build" your own library. Your selections can and should reflect your own tastes and interests, but try to make them wide and varied. Include some of the classics, contemporary fiction, poetry, and biography.

Save your high school and college texts—you'll be amazed at how some of the material retains its relevance. And try to read a good newspaper every day to keep current and informed.

Chapter 4

Maximize your Memory

"You should always be taking pictures, if not with a camera then with your mind. Memories you capture on purpose are always more vivid than the ones you pick up by accident."

—Isaac Marion

I could make a pretty good case that whatever time you invest improving your memory will deliver the most "study bang" for your buck. It doesn't matter how rapidly you whiz through your textbooks if you can't even remember the subject you studied...five minutes later. Getting organized is essential, but not if you always forget to turn in homework assignments or miss quizzes. And, of course, spending hours searching high and low for keys, glasses, your cellphone, and other essentials isn't the most efficient way to start your study day.

As important as they are, basic memory techniques are the study ingredients *least* likely to be taught in schools, even in a study skills course. So while many schools and teachers might help you with reading, writing, organizing, and test strategies, far too many of them will still "forget" to help you with your memory.

Retention, recall, and recognition

The essence of memory is the ability to get in touch with some fact or sensation *as if it had just happened.* Developing a skilled or practiced memory is to keep facts, formulas, and experiences at your disposal so you can recall them whenever you need or want to.

Why do so many of us forget where we put our car keys, eyeglasses, or cellphones? Because putting these objects down is the most ordinary of occurrences, part and parcel of the most humdrum aspects of our lives. (According to *Readers Digest*, the average adult spends *16 hours a year* trying to find his or her keys.) We have trouble remembering facts and formulas from books and classroom lectures for the same reason. To be in school is to be bombarded with information day in and day out. How do you make those facts memorable? (And has anyone seen my glasses?)

What do all "memorable" names, dates, places, and events have in common? The fact that they're *different*. What makes something memorable is its *extra*ordinariness, how much it differs from our normal experiences.

So how can some people so easily recite the names, symbols, and atomic weights of the elements of the periodic table—while they're playing (and winning) Trivial Pursuit?

Because this information has gotten "tagged" or "coded" in some way. For some people, myriad bits of data are almost automatically tagged so that they can be quite easily and handily stored and retrieved. But most of us, if we are to have exceptional memories, must make a special effort.

Let's explore how our memories actually work. There are three key processes involved—retention, recall, and recognition—and three major kinds of memory—visual, verbal, and kinesthetic.

If something is important enough

Retention is the process by which we keep imprints of past experiences in our minds, the "storage depot." Subject to other actions of the mind, what is retained can be recalled when needed. Things are retained in the same order in which they are learned. So your studying should build one fact, one idea, or one concept upon another.

Broad concepts can be retained more easily than details. Master generalities and details will fall into place.

If you think something is important, you will retain it more easily. So convincing yourself that what you are studying is something you must retain (and recall) increases your chances of adding it to your storehouse—your long-term memory bank.

Retention is primarily a product of what you understand. It has little to do with how *fast* you read, how great an outline you can construct, or how many fluorescent colors you use to highlight your textbooks. Reading a text, grasping the message, and remembering it are the fundamentals that make for high-level retention. Reading at a one thousand-word-per-minute clip does not necessarily mean that you understand what you read or will remember any of it.

As you work toward improving your reading, realize that speed is secondary to comprehension. If you can read an assignment faster than anyone in class, but can't give a one-sentence synopsis of what you just read, you've wasted your time. If you really get the author's message—even if it takes you an hour or two longer than some of your friends—spending the time you require to actually understand what you are reading will pay huge dividends in class and later in life.

It's on the tip of my tongue

Recall is the process by which we are able to bring forth those things that we have retained. Recall is subject to strengthening through the process of repetition. *Recall is least effective immediately after a first reading,* which is why reviewing the material later is so essential. The dynamics of our ability to recall are affected by several factors:

> We most easily recall those things that are of interest to us.

> Be selective in determining how much you need to recall. All information is not of equal importance—focus your attention on being able to recall the most *important* pieces of information.

> Allow yourself to react to what you're studying. Associating new information with what you already know will make it easier to recall.

> Repeat, either aloud or in your mind, what you want to remember. Find new ways to say those things that you want to recall.

> Try to recall broad concepts rather than isolated facts.

> Use the new data you have managed to recall in a meaningful way—it will help you recall it the next time.

Don't I know you from somewhere?

Recognition is the ability to see new material and recognize it for what it is and what it means. Familiarity is the key aspect of recognition—you will feel that you have "met" this information before, associate it with other data or circumstances, then recall the framework in which it logically fits.

If you've ever envied a friend's seemingly wondrous ability to recall facts, dates, and telephone numbers virtually at will, take solace that, in most cases, *this skill is a result of study and practice*, not a talent he inherited.

Why we forget

As you think about the elements of developing good memory, you can use them to address why you *forget*. The root of poor memory is usually found in one of these areas:

> We fail to make the material meaningful
> We did not learn prerequisite material
> We fail to grasp what is to be remembered
> We do not have the desire to remember
> We allow apathy or boredom to dictate how we learn
> We have no set habit for learning
> We are disorganized and inefficient in our use of study time
> We do not use the knowledge we have gained

And more ways to remember

Here are some additional hints that will help you remember what you read:

> You will remember only what you *understand*. When you read something and grasp the

message, you have begun the process of retention. The way to test this is to rephrase the message in your own words. Can you summarize
the main idea? Unless you understand what is
being said, you won't be able to decide whether
to remember or discard it.

> You remember what you *choose* to remember.
If you don't want to remember some piece of
information or don't believe you *can,* then you
won't! To remember the material, you must *want*
to remember it and be convinced that you *will*
remember it.

> To ensure that you retain material, you need
to go beyond simply doing the assignment. To
really remember what you learn, you should
learn material thoroughly, or *over*learn. This
involves pre-reading the text, doing a critical read, and having some definite means of
review that reinforces what you should have
learned.

> It's more difficult to remember random thoughts
or numbers than those organized in some pattern. For example, which phone number is
easier to remember: 538-6284 or 678-1234?
Once you *recognize the pattern* in the second
number, it takes much less effort to remember
than the first. Develop the ability to discern the
structure that exists and recall it when you try
to remember. Have a system to help you recall
how information is organized and connected.

> It's helpful to attach or *associate* what you are
trying to recall to something already in your
memory. Mentally link new material to existing

knowledge so that you are giving this new thought some context in your mind.

Three kinds of memory

They are visual, verbal, and kinesthetic, *each* of which can be strong or weak and only the first two of which are associated with your *brain*. This is, of course, a gross simplification of what we term "memory." Surveys have found more than a hundred different memory tasks in everyday life that can cause people problems, each of which requires a different strategy! Sorry to break it to you, but just because you've learned an easy way to remember a 100-digit number (see the end of this chapter) does *not* guarantee that you won't still spend days looking for those darned glasses.

Most people have the easiest time strengthening their *visual* memories, which is why so many memory techniques involve forming "mental pictures."

To strengthen our verbal memories, we use rhymes, songs, letter substitutions, and other mnemonic gimmicks.

Finally, don't underestimate the importance of kinesthetic memory, or what your *body* remembers. Athletes and dancers certainly don't have to be convinced that the muscles, joints, and tendons of their bodies seem to have their own memories. Neither does anyone who's ever remembered a phone number by moving his fingers and "remembering" how it's dialed.

The next time you have to remember a list, any list, say each item out loud and move some part of your body at the same time. A tap dancer can do the time step and remember her history lecture. A baseball pitcher can associate each movement of his windup with another item of a list he has to memorize. Even random body movements will do.

For example, if you have to memorize a list of countries, just associate each one with a specific movement. For Botswana, say it aloud while lifting your right arm. For Zimbabwe, rotate your neck. Bend a knee for Lesotho, and raise your left hand for Burkina Faso. Kick Malawi in the shins and twirl your hair for Mauritius. Touch your right big toe for Kyrgyzstan, your left big toe for Kazakhstan; bend your left pinkie for Tajikistan and your right for Turkmenistan.

When you have to remember this list of countries, just start moving! It may look a little strange—especially if you make your movements a little too exotic or dramatic in the middle of geography class—but if it works for *you*, who cares?

You can also use this newfound memory as a backup to your brain. You'll probably find that even if you forget the "mental" tricks you used, your "body memory" will run (or lift or squat or bend or shake) to the rescue!

Tag, you're it!

As we said at the beginning of this chapter, we need to establish tags or codes for items we wish to remember so that our minds will have relatively little difficulty retrieving them from long-term memory.

The "chain link" method is one of the methods used for "tagging" items *before they enter* that morass of memory. It will help you remember items that appear in sequence, whether it's the association of a date with an event, a scientific term with its meaning, or other facts or objects that are supposed to "go together."

The basis for the chain-link system is that memory works best when you associate the unfamiliar with the familiar, though sometimes the association may be very odd. But to really make it effective, the odder the better.

Every Good Boy has a FACE

One of the simplest methods is to try to remember just the first letter of a sequence. That's how "Roy G. Biv" (the colors of the spectrum, in order from left to right—red, orange, yellow, green, blue, indigo, violet) got famous. Or "Every Good Boy Does Fine," to remember the notes on a musical staff. Or, perhaps the simplest of all, "FACE," to remember the notes in between.

Of course, not many sequences work out as nicely as HOMES, an effective way to remember the Great Lakes (Huron, Ontario, Michigan, Erie, and Superior). If you tried to memorize the signs of the Zodiac with this method, you'd wind up with (A)ries, (T)aurus, (G)emini, (C)ancer, (L)eo, (V)irgo, (L)ibra, (S)corpio, (S)agittarius, (C)apricorn, (A)quarius, (P)isces. Now maybe you can make a name or a place or something out of ATGCLVLSSCAP, but I can't!

One solution is to make up a simple sentence that uses the first letters of the list you're trying to remember as the first letters of each word, creating a brief but more memorable story. For example, "**A T**ipsy **G**erbil **C**hased **L**ions, **V**ipers, and **L**eopards while **S**ome **S**toned **C**ows **A**te **P**opcorn."

Wait a minute! That story is two words longer than the list of zodiacal signs. Why not just figure out some way to memorize the Zodiac? What's better about the second set? First of all, it's easier (and definitely more fun) to picture a drunken gerbil chasing predators and a stoned cow eating popcorn. As we'll soon see, creating such mental images is a very powerful way to remember almost anything. Second, because the words in our sentence have formed at least two distinct pictures, they're much easier to remember. Go ahead and try it yourself. See how long it takes you to memorize the sentence versus all the signs.

Remember: Make your sentence(s) memorable to *you*. *Any* sentence or series of words that helps you remember these letters will do. Here are just two more I created in a few seconds:

A Tall **G**iraffe **C**alled **L**as **V**egas **L**oved to **S**ip **S**odas from **C**ans **A**nd **P**lates.

Any **T**iny **G**erm **C**ould **L**ove **V**enus. **L**ong **S**ilk **S**nakes **C**ould **A**ll **P**ray.

Isn't it easy to make up silly, memorable pictures in your head for these?

There is a limit to this technique however: Unless the list itself is familiar to you (like the colors of the spectrum or signs of the Zodiac), this method will do you little good. For example, medical students for decades have used the mnemonic **O**n **O**ld **O**lympia's **T**owering **T**op **A F**inn **A**nd **G**erman **V**ault **A**nd **H**op to remember the list of cranial nerves: olfactory, optic, oculomotor, trochlear, trigeminal, abducens, facial, auditory, glossopharyngeal, vagus, accessory, and hypoglossal). The only way the letter "G" in "German" is going to remind you of "glossopharyngeal" is if you have already spent a significant amount of time studying (memorizing?) this list!

Let's try another example, one with which I doubt most of you are at all familiar—the months of the Islamic calendar: Mohorran, Safar, Rabi I, Rabi II, Jumada I, Jumada II, Rajab, Shaban, Ramadan, Shawwal, Dhu 'l-Qada, and Dhu 'l-hijjah.

Here's the way I would remember these months.

I'm in the desert, on a *safari*, with *two rabbis*, Joe and Ben. (Whew! Three months in one sentence!) We decide to stop and eat. I held up *two* big sandwiches and tried to *show* them to *Ben*, but he got *mad* that *Joe* hadn't used enough meat. *"More ham,"* he cried, which was a very strange thing for a rabbi to yell. Before I knew it, Joe had thrown a *right jab* at Ben. Luckily, we noticed a *Ramada* Inn right up ahead, with a huge, blue genie wearing a *shawl* standing in front of it. But Ben was still mad. Joe, I challenge you to a *duel*, you *cad.* "Oh, yeah," cried Joe, as he *hitched up* his robes. "Well, I challenge you to a *duel, too.*

Remember, it's not enough to memorize this kind of story and use the words as triggers for your memory. You must create the picture in your mind—the two rabbis on camels, the sandwich that needs more ham, the right jab thrown by Joe, the Ramada Inn in the middle of the desert with a genie in front. Make each of them stand out in your mind. Perhaps the genie looks like your grandmother, what with the shawl and all. Perhaps the ham is green (presuming you're a Dr. Seuss fan). Whatever it takes to make *your* pictures easily recallable and memorable.

Now you try. Here is another obscure list—two dozen ancient British kings:

Octavius, Constantius, Sulgenius, Eliud, Redon, Eldol, Heli, Lud, Penessil, Idvallo, Millus, Archgallo, Pir, Brutus, Maddan, Hud, Hudibras, Gorboduc, Porrex, Danius, Ingenius, Keredic, Cadvan, Vortimer.

Time yourself. When you can construct a series of pictures to remember a list like this—and remember it for a while, not just a day—all in less than five minutes, you are well on your way to mastering this powerful memory technique.

Here are four more lists to practice with:

Cheeses: Samsoe, caboc, stracchino, Red Windsor, Hram Sag, Esrom, Vacherin, Wexford, Provolone, sapsago, Crowdie, Pultost, Arran, Blarney, Mysost, Islay.

Ships or vessels: Drake, saic, butty, shallop, grab, brigantine, carrack, pram, bawley, whiff, packet, budgerow, gallivant, dogger, Geordie, randan, drake, monoxylon.

Unusual fruits and vegetables: yangmei, dudhi, manioc, karela, garlic scape, durian, loofah, cherimoya, pummelo, jabuticaba, samphire, dulse, gai lan, santol, langsat, atemoya, rollinia, pitaya, canistel, kalamansi.

Dances: Maxixe, Cabriole, Doppio, Saltarello, Estampie, Polonaise, Bergamask, Ketjak, Moresco, Tordion, Kazachoc, Juba, Safabaude, Zambra, Farruga, Galliard, Czardas, Bourree, Matachin.

Clearly you don't have to *understand* what you are trying to memorize or even the correct way to pronounce the obscure elements of a list (though correct spelling and, in some stories you will create, the order of items will be important).

Here are four ways to create chain links that will help you remember almost anything:

> To the extent possible, make the chain-link scenarios you construct highly *unusual*.
> Don't think of an object just sitting there. Have it *do something*—the crazier the better.
> Conjure up a scenario that elicits an *emotional reaction*—joy, sorrow, physical pain, whatever.
> Many lessons for preschoolers and those in first and second grades are done with *rhymes*. If it works for them, it should work for you, right?
> If you've taken trigonometry, you probably learned the acronym of Chief SOH-CAH-TOA, an easy way to remember that Sine equals

Opposite/Hypotenuse; Cosine equals Adjacent/ Hypotenuse; and Tangent equals Opposite/ Adjacent.

The mnemonic alphabet

Up until now, we've been dealing in the rich world of words. Anything having to do with words is a relatively easy task for the memory because words always can be associated with *things*. And things, because they can be seen, touched, heard, and smelled, can carry more than one association and, therefore, be easier to remember.

But a number is an abstraction. Unless associated with something, it is relatively difficult to remember. For instance, most people have tremendous difficulty remembering telephone numbers that they've only heard once. The reason is that a phone number doesn't usually conjure up an image or a sensation. It is merely a bunch of digits without a relationship to one another or to you.

The trick, then, is to establish more associations for numbers.

But how? After all, they can be so abstract. It would be like trying to remember colors without having the benefit of *things* associated with those colors.

Making friends with numbers

Numbers are infinite, but the system we use to designate them is even more user-friendly than the alphabet. It consists of 10 digits that all of you should know by now (just follow the bouncing ball): 0, 1, 2, 3, 4, 5, 6, 7, 8, and 9.

The trick to the mnemonic alphabet—a rather popular technique for remembering numbers—is turning those numbers into the equivalent of letters, symbols that represent sounds. The pioneer of this concept is Harry Lorayne, author of many books on memory. His method calls for associating the 10 familiar Arabic numerals with a sound or a related group of sounds.

Here's how this brilliantly simple scheme works:

1 = T, D	6 = J, soft G, CH, SH
2 = N	7 = K, hard C, hard G, Q
3 = M	8 = F, V, PH
4 = R	9 = P, B
5 = L	0 = Z, soft C, S

You're probably thinking, "What sense does this all make, and how in the heck am I supposed to remember it or use it?"

Well, though this seems like madness, believe me, there's an extraordinarily wonderful method in it.

The number one is a single down stroke, as is the letter "T." "D" is a suitable substitute because it is pronounced almost the same way as "T"—by touching the tongue to the front of the roof of the mouth.

"N" represents two because "N" has two down strokes.

"M" is a stand-in for three because, you guessed it, it has three down strokes.

Four is represented by "R" because the dominant sound in the word *four* is the "-rrrrr" at the end.

The Romans used "L" to represent 50. Also, if you fan out the fingers of your left hand as if to say, "It is 5 o'clock," your index finger and thumb form the letter "L."

Hold a mirror up to a six and you get a "J," particularly if you write as badly as I do. Therefore, all letters pronounced like "J"—by touching your tongue to the inside of your lower teeth—are acceptable substitutes for six.

Place two sevens back to back, turning one upside down, and what do you have? Right, a "K." All letter sounds formed in the back of the mouth, as is "K," are therefore potential substitutes for the lucky seven.

Draw a line parallel to the ground through a handwritten eight and you will create a symbol that resembles a script, lower case "F." Therefore, all sounds formed by placing the top teeth on the lower lip can represent eight.

Once again, a mirror will show you that a nine and a capital "P" are virtually identical. "B," also formed by putting your lips together, is a substitute for nine anytime.

Zero is an easy one. It begins with a "Z," so any sound formed by hissing through the space between a flat tongue and the roof of your mouth is acceptable.

Lorayne reminds us that what's important is the *sounds* these letters make. That's why, when using mnemonics, you assign no numerical value to silent letters nor to doubled consonants (two "tt's" is the same sound as one), unless each of the letters *sounds* differently (for example, accessory).

Have you noticed that all of the letters used in the mnemonic alphabet are consonants? That's because users of the system are free to use vowels however they please around these consonants to form words or memorable sounds. Therefore the number 85 can be FooL. Or the number of that wonderful person you met in the Student Center today and would so like to see again could be a "normal girl," or 243-5475 (NRMLGRL).

How about trying to remember pi to seven places? You could try to memorize 3.141592 or just think, "MeTRic TalL PeNny." Is it easier to remember your social security number (say, 143-25-7170) or "DooRMeN LiKe DoGS."

What about even longer numbers? How do you remember 20-, 30-, even 50-digit numbers without trying too hard?

Well, you could make your "story sentences" longer. But you can also group the numbers into a series of pictures.

For example, let's say you had to remember the number 289477500938199101550. That's 21 digits! Try grouping it into smaller number combinations, creating a picture for each:

289477 can be represented by NVPRGK or a picture of a sailor (NaVy) PouRing GunK.

500938 is LZZBMV. The sailor is standing LaZily, right By a Movie Theater.

199101550. What's playing at the theater? DeBBie DoeS DallaS.

Can you see how you could memorize a 50-digit number with just four or five pictures? Try it yourself. You'll see how easy it is.

Other ways to use mnemonics

This powerful system is not just for remembering long numbers. Here is a list of U.S. vice-presidents since World War II:

34 Harry Truman
35 Alben Barkley
36 Richard Nixon
37 Lyndon Johnson
38 Hubert Humphrey
39 Spiro Agnew
40 Gerald Ford
41 Nelson Rockefeller
42 Walter Mondale
43 George H. W. Bush
44 Dan Quayle
45 Al Gore

46 Dick Cheney
47 Joe Biden

Here's how you could you use mnemonics to establish a chain link between the names and corresponding numbers:

Truman: Meet MR (34) True, man
Quayle: Picture a RoaRing (44) quail
Mondale: Picture a Jamaican Ayrdale (mon) RuNning (42)
Ford: Picture a brand new Ford truck RiSing (40) in the air.

Where to hang your memory

Another mnemonic memory method is the Peg Word System, which assigns a different word to numbers 1 through 10. Harry's peg words don't need to be memorized since they're based on the mnemonic alphabet you already learned:

The Peg Word System

1. Tie
2. Noah
3. Ma
4. Rye
5. Law
6. Shoe
7. Cow
8. Ivy
9. Bee
10. Toes

When you have to remember a list in order or associate a number with some other information (such as vice presidents of the United States), you can use these peg words for the numbers. Mr. Lorayne has even extended the list to 100, utilizing words such as mummy (33), cage (76), roof (48), and dozes (100).

It's certainly possible to create your own peg word system utilizing the sounds of the mnemonic alphabet (though why reinvent the wheel Harry already designed?). Alternatively, you can utilize a completely different basic peg word system cited by author Dr. Fiona McPherson in her book *The Memory Key*. While not associating it to the sounds used in the mnemonic alphabet, using a rhyme scheme makes it equally memorable:

1. Bun
2. Shoe
3. Tree
4. Door
5. Hive
6. Sticks (or Bricks)
7. Heaven
8. Gate
9. Line
10. Hen

As I have emphasized throughout this book, use whichever method or list of peg words you find easiest, or go ahead and create your own!

Chapter 5

Manage your **Time**

"Those who make the worst use of their time are the first to complain of its brevity."

—Jean de la Bruyere

I'm sure many of you reading this are struggling with sometimes overwhelming responsibilities and commitments. Some of you may be so burned out that you've just given up. Those of you who haven't probably figure it's your fault—if you just worked *harder* and spent *more* time studying—then everything would work out just fine.

So you resign yourselves to caffeine-fueled all-nighters, cramming for tests, and forgetting about time-consuming activities like eating and sleeping. Trying to do everything—even when there's too much to do—without acquiring the skills to *control* your time, is an approach that will surely lead to frustration and failure.

Whatever your current challenges, a simple, easy-to-follow organizational system is crucial to your success. And despite your natural inclination to proclaim that you just don't have the *time* to spend scheduling, listing, and recording, it's also the best way to give yourself *more* time.

You *can* plan ahead and make conscious choices about how your time will be spent and how much time you will spend on each task. You *can* have more control over your time, rather than always running out of it.

The first step for efficiently managing your time is to decide what is important...and what isn't. Difficult as it may be, sometimes it's necessary for us to recognize that we truly *can't* do it all, that we must eliminate anything from our busy schedules that *isn't* as important to us so we can devote more energy to the tasks that are.

There *is* enough time to plan

Even after paring down our commitments, most of us are still challenged to accomplish everything we should or want to. With classes, study time, work, extracurricular activities, and a social life, it's not easy fitting it all in.

The organizational plan that I outline in this chapter is designed particularly for students. Whether you're in high school, college, or graduate school, a "traditional" student or one who's returning to school, you'll find that this is a manageable program that will work for you.

This program allows for flexibility. In fact, I encourage you to adapt any of my recommendations to your own unique needs. That means it will work for you whether you are living in a dorm, sharing accommodations with a roommate, or living with a spouse and children.

The purpose of this chapter is to help you make *choices* about what is important to you, set *goals* for yourself, *organize* and *schedule* your time, and develop the *motivation* and *self-discipline* to follow your schedule and reach those goals.

Why take the time?

An organizational or time-management system that fits your needs can help you get more work done in less time. Whether your priority is more free time, improved grades, a less frantic life—or all of the above—learning how to organize your life and your studies can help you reach your objective, because an effective time-management system:

> *Helps you put first things first.* Have you ever spent an evening doing a time-consuming assignment for an *easy* class, only to find that you hadn't spent enough time studying for a crucial test in a more difficult one?

> *Helps you learn how long everything really takes.* One of the important components of this system is estimating how long each task will take you and tracking how long you actually spend doing it. Once you've inculcated this concept into your life, you'll finally discover where all that time you've been "losing" has been going.

> *Reduces your tendency to procrastinate.* Once you have a realistic idea of the specific things you must accomplish and know that you have allocated sufficient time to finish them, you're less likely to get frustrated and put them off.

> *Helps you avoid time traps.* Time traps are the fires you have to put out before you can turn to

tasks like studying. Time management is like
a fire-*prevention* approach rather than a fire-
fighting one: It allows you to go about your work
systematically instead of moving from crisis to
crisis or whim to whim.

> *Helps you anticipate opportunities.* In addition
to helping you balance study time with other
time demands, effective time management can
help make the time you *do* spend studying more
productive.

> *Gives you freedom and control.* Contrary to many
students' fears, time management is *liberating*, not
restrictive. A certain control over *part* of your day
allows you to be flexible with the *rest* of your day.

> *Helps you avoid time conflicts.* Simply having all
of your activities, assignments, appointments,
errands, and reminders in *one* place helps
ensure that two or three things don't get scheduled at once. If time conflicts do arise, you will
notice them well in advance and be able to rearrange things accordingly.

> *Helps you avoid feeling guilty.* It is much easier
to forget about studying if you've already allotted
the time for it. Without a plan to finish the work
you are doing, you may feel like it's "hanging over
your head"—even when you're not working on it.

> *Helps you evaluate your progress.* If you know
you have to read an average of 75 pages a week
to keep up in your business management class,
and you've only read 60 pages this week, you
don't need a calculator to figure out that you are
slightly behind. And it's easy enough to schedule
a little more time to read next week so you can
catch up.

> *Helps you see the big picture.* Effective time management provides you with a bird's-eye view of the semester. Instead of being caught off guard when the busy times come, you will be able to plan ahead—*weeks* ahead—when you have big tests or assignments due in more than one class.

> *Helps you see the bigger picture.* Planning ahead and plotting your course early allows you to see how classes fit with your overall school career.

> *Helps you learn how to study smarter, not harder.* You may become *so* organized, *so* prioritized, *so in control of your time,* that you can spend *less* time studying, get *better* grades, and have *more* time for other things—extracurricular activities, hobbies, whatever.

Time management is *not* magic, though it can *appear* magical.

Identify the starting line

You can't race off to your ultimate goal until you figure out where your starting line is. So the first step necessary to overhaul your current routine is to *identify* it. There are two ways to go about this; I suggest you do both.

The first is to use the chart on the next page to assess how much time you actually have available for studying. If it's clearly not enough, then you'd better reassess how much time you're spending in each of the other areas. You may have to cut your part-time work hours, quit a club, even change your schedule to reduce your commute. Of course, if you're spending two hours a day on "grooming" or three hours eating, the solution may be a little more obvious.

Create a second chart yourself. Write down, in 15-minute increments, how you spend your time *right now*. While keeping track of all your activities for a day or two might be sufficient for some of you, I recommend you chart them for an entire week, including the weekend.

This is especially important if, like many people, you have huge pockets of time that seemingly disappear, but in reality are devoted to things like "resting" after you wake up, putting on makeup or shaving, reading the paper, or waiting for transportation. Could you use an extra hour or two a day, either for studying or for fun? Make better use of such "dead" time and you'll find all the time you need.

Where Does Your Time Go?

	Hrs./Day	Days/Wk.	Hrs./Wk.
Meals (including prep and cleanup)	_____	7	_____
Sleeping (including naps)	_____	7	_____
Grooming	_____	7	_____
Commuting	_____	5?	_____
Errands	_____	7	_____
Extracurricular activities	_____	_____	_____
Part- or full-time job	_____	_____	_____
In class	_____	_____	_____
Entertainment*	_____	_____	_____

*Hanging with friends, going out, watching TV, reading for pleasure, etc.

Fill in the first column, multiply by the second, then total the third column. There are 168 hours in a week (24 x 7). How many do you currently have left for studying? Note: Any answer that contains a minus is a *bad* sign.

Learn how to do multiple tasks at the same time: Listen to an audiobook while you're puttering around the house; practice vocabulary or math drills while you're driving; or have your kids, parents, or roommates quiz you for an upcoming test while you're doing the dishes, vacuuming, or gardening. And *always* carry some study materials (a textbook, term paper outline, or flashcards) with you—you can get a phenomenal amount of reading or studying done while in line or on a bus or train.

Strategy tip: Identify those items on your calendar, whatever their priority, that you could complete in 15 minutes or less. These are the ideal tasks to tackle during any "dead" time.

Collect what you need

As you begin your planning session, make sure you have all of the information and materials you need to make a quality plan. Gather your class syllabuses; work schedule; dates of important family events, vacations, or trips; other personal commitments (doctor's appointments, exercise classes, dates and parties); and the calendars of any extracurricular events in which you plan to participate.

The two items you need to become the most organized person you know are a long-term planning calendar and a more detailed daily calendar.

How to keep track of your day-to-day activities (classes, appointments, regular daily homework assignments, and daily or weekly quizzes) will be dealt with a little later in this chapter. First, let's discuss those projects—studying for midterms and finals, term papers, theses—that require completion over a longer period of time, weeks, maybe even months.

This long-term planning calendar will not contain a great amount of detail. Rather, it should function as an overview of your schedule for an entire quarter or semester, a kind of "life-at-a-glance" summary. So just enter the date of every quiz or test, when papers and projects are due, important future appointments (it's not just for schoolwork), and anything else you must remember.

Since this calendar ideally needs to show three or four months at a time, I still prefer (and recommend that you use) an old-fashioned wall calendar. Its very size makes it easy to recognize and remember events or assignments scheduled weeks or even months in the future.

I have reproduced a sample copy of a long-term planning calendar on p. 131. As you can see, there is little detail included—just enough to remind one, for example, not to schedule a date for January 6th or expect to get much studying done the weekend of the 20th.

I need to acknowledge here that for most of us, the days of printed "Week at a Glance" calendars are long gone. There are now a wide variety of online calendars available for use on whatever mobile device you choose. Google Calendar, iCal, and Microsoft Outlook may be the current favorites, but there are hundreds if not thousands more from which to choose. Most allow for detailed customization, letting you choose formats, colors, fonts, and much more. Calendar and organizing apps for your smartphone—including to-do lists, reminders and alerts—are even more prevalent.

In the rest of this chapter, I will describe the steps you need to take to become more organized. It is completely up to you, as I've emphasized, what specific tools you choose to use. High school students may find it quite easy to use only their smartphone calendar app, as they are usually not subject to quite as many long-term projects as college or graduate students.

I have personally transitioned to keeping my entire calendar and daily to-do lists on my iPhone, since it is always (unfortunately) with me. Many of you may not see the need for this second calendar either and just keep your schedules and reminders on your phone and/or computer.

Again, the format doesn't matter; the principles do. All of the details of your life should be included on your daily calendar, wherever you keep it.

Choose your calendar

I have reproduced a sample daily calendar on pp. 132 and 133.

Your calendar must contain everything you need to do this week. If you are utilizing a long-term calendar, be sure you have transferred over details of any school-related tasks. Add any other tasks that must be done this week, from sending off a birthday present to your sister, attending your monthly volunteer meeting, or finding the time to do laundry or buy groceries.

Remember to break any long-term or difficult projects into small, "bite-size" tasks that can be included on your schedule. As Henry Ford said, "Nothing is particularly hard if you divide it into small jobs." Hence, the assembly line.

Whatever actual format you use, I would recommend your calendar contains these key elements, as I've indicated on my sample:

> Every assignment due that week ("Geometry problems" on the 20th, 21st, and 24th; "History reading" for the 20th and 22nd).
> Every task that is a step in a longer-term assignment ("Choose an English topic" on the 20th; "study for History mid-term" on February 3rd).
> All non-homework chores, appointments, phone calls, and so on.
> A code (I've used A, B, C) that prioritizes each task.
> An estimate (under "T" in my sample) of the amount of time allocated to each task.
> The actual time ("A") each task took.
> Any additional notes or reminders ("bring gym shorts," "call mom!").

Remind me again, why do all this?

I think prioritizing your tasks is extremely important. When you sit down to study without a plan, you just dive into the first project that comes to mind. Of course, there's no guarantee that the first thing that comes to mind will be the most important. The point of using some sort of code to prioritize tasks is to arrange them *in order of importance.* That way, even if you find yourself without enough time for everything, you can at least finish those assignments that are most important.

If you push aside the same low-priority item day after day, week after week, at some point you should just stop and decide whether it's something you need to do at all! This is a strategic way to make a task or problem "disappear." In the business world, some managers purposefully avoid confronting problems, waiting to see which will simply resolve themselves through benign neglect. If it works in business, it can work for you in school.

I also like the idea of estimating time and how long actually took. Whatever total time you wind up allocating should approximate the time you actually have available. If you find yourself habitually spending more time on assignments than you have projected, consider adding a "safety margin" to your estimates. Then total all the estimates and make sure you haven't scheduled yourself until 4 a.m.!

Getting into this habit will make you more aware of how much time to allocate to future projects and make sure that the more you do so, the more accurate your estimates will be.

The more time you have to complete a project, the easier it is to procrastinate, even to delay identifying the steps and entering them into your regular schedule. If you find yourself leaving long-term projects to the last week, schedule the projects furthest away—the term paper due in three months, the oral exam 10 weeks from now—*first*. Then trick yourself—schedule the completion date at least seven days prior to the actual turn-in date, giving yourself a one-week cushion for life's inevitable surprises. (Just try to forget you've used this trick. Otherwise, you'll be like the perennial latecomer who set his watch 15 minutes fast—except he always reminded himself to add 15 minutes to the time on his wrist, undoing his strategy.)

Besides the importance of the task and the available time you have to complete it, other factors will determine how you utilize these tools. Some will be beyond your control: work schedules, appointments with professors, counselors, and doctors, and so on. But there are plenty of factors you *do* control, which you should consider as you plan your schedule.

Don't overdo it. Plan your study time in blocks, breaking up work time with short leisure activities. It's helpful to add these to your schedule as well. You'll find that these breaks help you think more clearly and creatively when you get back to studying.

Even if you tend to like longer blocks of study time, be careful about scheduling study "marathons"—six- or eight-hour stretches rather than a series of two-hour sessions. The longer the period you schedule, the more likely you'll have to fight the demons of procrastination and fatigue. Convincing yourself that you are really studying your heart out, you'll also find it easier to justify time-wasting distractions, scheduling longer breaks, and, before long, quitting before you should.

Remember Parkinson's Law: Work expands so as to fill the time available for its completion. In other words, if you fail to schedule a one-hour block for a project that *should* take an hour, you will probably be surprised to find that (eureka!) it somehow takes two or three.

Using these tools effectively

Once you have discovered habits and patterns of study that work for you, continue to use and hone them. Be flexible enough to add techniques you learn from others and practical enough to alter schedules that circumstances have made obsolete.

Plan according to *your* schedule, *your* goals, and *your* aptitudes, not some ephemeral "standard." Allocate the time you expect a project to take *you*, not the time it might take someone else or how long your teacher says it should take. Try to be realistic and honest with yourself when determining those things that require more effort or those that come easier to you.

Whenever possible, schedule pleasurable activities *after* study time, not before. They will then act as incentives, not distractions.

Monitor your progress at reasonable periods and make changes where necessary. This is *your* study regimen—you conceived it, you can change it. If you find that you are consistently allotting more time than necessary to a specific chore, change your future schedule accordingly.

As assignments are entered on your calendar, make sure you also enter items needed—texts; other books you have to buy, borrow, or get from the library; and materials such as drawing pads, magic markers, and graph paper.

Adapt these tools for your own use. Try anything you think may work—use it if it does, discard it if it doesn't.

Try doing your *least* favorite chores (study assignments, projects, whatever) first—you'll feel better having gotten them out of the way! And plan how to accomplish them as meticulously as possible. That will get rid of them even faster.

If you see that you are moving along faster than you anticipated on one task or project sequence, there is absolutely nothing wrong with continuing onto the next part of that assignment or the next project step.

If you're behind, don't panic. Just reorganize your schedule and find the time you need to make up.

Write things down. Not having to remember all these items will free up space in your brain for the things you need to concentrate on or *do* have to remember.

Learn to manage distractions. As a time management axiom puts it, "Don't respond to the urgent and forget the important." Some things you do can be picked up or dropped at any time. Beware of those time-consuming and complicated tasks that, once begun, demand to be completed. Being interrupted at any point might mean starting all over again. What a waste of time *that* would be!

Nothing can be as counterproductive as losing your concentration, especially at critical times. Learn to ward off those enemies that would alter your course and you will find your journey much smoother.

One way to guard against these mental intrusions is to know your own study clock and plan accordingly. Each of us is predisposed to function most efficiently at specific times of the day (or night). Find out what sort of study clock you are on and schedule your work accordingly.

Beware of uninvited guests: Unless you are ready for a break, they'll only lure you off schedule. More subtle enemies include the sudden desire to sharpen every pencil in the house, an unheard-of urge to clean your room, or an offer to do your sister's homework. If you find yourself doing anything *but* your own work, either take a break then and there or pull yourself together and get down to work. Self-discipline, too, is a learned habit that gets easier with practice.

The simple act of saying no (to others or to yourself) will help insulate you from these unwelcome interruptions. Put your "Do not disturb" sign up and stick to your guns, no matter what the temptations.

And if your schedule involves working with others, take *their* sense of time into account—you may find you have to schedule "waiting time" for a chronically late friend...and always bring a book along.

A special note for commuters

If you live at home (as opposed to being housed on campus), there are some special pressures with which you need to contend.

Your commute to school will probably be longer than if you could just roll out of bed and walk to class. It will certainly require more wakefulness, even if you just have to stumble to a subway or bus (but especially if you have to drive!). It's especially important that you minimize travel time, planning enough to maximize your use of the campus facilities without having to schedule a trip home in between.

While nobody likes walking to class in rain, sleet, or snow—except, perhaps, future postal employees—it is invariably easier to walk a few tree-lined blocks than drive a few miles in inclement weather. Take weather problems into account when scheduling your commute.

The very act of living at home—whether as a child or one "married with children"—brings with it responsibilities to others you could minimize living in a dorm. Be ready to allocate time to these responsibilities and include them in your study schedule. They're as inevitable if you live at home as meatloaf on Tuesdays.

The most important 15 minutes of your day

Set aside 15 minutes every day to go over your daily and weekly priorities. While many businesspeople like to make this the first 15 minutes of their day, I recommend making it the *last* 15 minutes of yours. Why? Three great reasons:

1. *Your ideas will be fresher.* It's easier to analyze at the *end* of the day what you've accomplished... and haven't.

2. *It's a great way to end the day.* Even if your "study day" ends at 11 p.m., you'll feel fully prepared for the next day and ready to relax, anxiety-free.

3. *You'll get off to a great start the next morning.* If you use the morning to plan, it's easy to turn a 15-minute planning session into an hour of aimless "thinking." While others are fumbling for a cup of coffee, you'll be off and running!

Now here's your payoff

Anything—even school—will seem less overwhelming if you break your assignments into "bite-size" pieces...and you already know the flavor.

You will no longer worry about when you're going to get that paper done—you've already planned for it.

You'll accomplish everything you need to—one step at a time.

As you get used to managing your time, you'll quickly discover that you seem to have more time than ever before.

Long-term Calendar (Filled-in Sample)

MONTH: *January*

MON	TUE	WED	THU	FRI	SAT	SUN
1	2	3	4	5	6	7
	Gorbachev rough paper due			*French vocab quiz*	*mom visit*	↑
8	9	10	11	12	13	14
	English midterm	*Geometry midterm*	*History midterm*			
15	16	17	18	19	20	21
					Lacrosse tourney ↑	↑
22	23	24	25	26	27	28
		First 2 parts of French project due		*French vocab quiz*	*Lacrosse tourney* ↑	↑
29	30	31				

Daily Calendar (Filled-in Sample)

January

20	Monday		T	A	Notes
A	Geometry	probs 24–42 odd	40	60	pick up milk & eggs
A	History	Read Chap 3	30	40	Don't forget homework!
A	Biology	Finish lab report	60	25	
	Read CH. 8	30	25		
C	Choose English topic		20	15	
	Check with teacher		10	10	
A	Bring gym shorts tomorrow				
B	Call Cheryl right after sch.				
A	7PM Band rehearsal		120	180	

21	Tuesday		T	A	Notes
C	Health	Redo chart (due Fri)	30	20	
A	Geometry	24-42 Even	40	70	
B	Spanish	Essay rough draft	75	120	See Mr. Dawkins for
					Thursday Appt.
B	Band 6:30		120	150	

22	Wednesday		T	A	Notes
A	Spanish	Essay final draft	60	70	
	proof	30	30		
A	History	Chap 4	30	45	
B	Biology	Chap 9	30	45	
		probs p.112	50	30	

Daily Calendar (Filled-in Sample)

January

23	Thursday	T	A	Notes
A	Finalize Health chart, proof	20	40	
B	research English paper	120	0	2:30 Mr. Dawkins
	(online)			@ Lib. office
				Bring gym shorts!
				Dr. Gevens 5PM
	Band 6:30	60	150	

24	Friday	T	A	Notes
B	Geometry probs 85-110	50	90	
				Jerry - Are u picking me
				up tonight?
				What time?
				Bring PJs
Call:	Rob 742-6891			Toothbrush
	Jack 742-2222			Makeup
	Ira 743-8181			CDs (see list)
	Cheryl 777-7777			

25	Saturday	T	A	Notes
A	Study for Geometry quiz	120	90	
B	Study for Hist. midterm	120	120	
	(Feb 3)			
A	Biology probs pp. 113-114	60	45	

26	Sunday	T	A	Notes
	ENJOY!			
				Call mom!
	Church 11AM			
	Brunch @ Amy's 2PM			

Chapter 6

Excel in **Class**

Most of your teachers will utilize the classroom setting to embellish and interpret material covered in the text and other assigned readings. If you always complete your reading assignments before class, you'll be able to devote your classroom time to the new material the teacher will undoubtedly cover.

She may well be covering it in exciting new ways. Technology is adding new tools to your teacher's arsenal at a breathless pace. Some of you may still spend your day in a traditional classroom your grandmother would surely recognize, with a chalk-covered blackboard, pull-down maps and projection screen, and an old overhead projector on its cart.

But many other classrooms have been radically transformed and boast interactive white boards, notebook computers instead of notebooks, and PowerPoint slide shows. And you may have evolved as well—I'm sure many of you now prefer a laptop or tablet to pen and paper.

The only downside I see in this ever evolving "wired classroom" is the sheer overload of information it can produce.

Otherwise, such technological developments have just made many of the lessons included in this chapter easier to implement—you can access PowerPoint slides, your teacher's notes and suggested reading, even his or her detailed website—anytime, anywhere.

It doesn't particularly matter *how* the information you need to learn is conveyed, as long as you develop the necessary skills to access it, analyze it, and retain it.

Class distinctions

Exactly how you'll use the skills we'll cover in this chapter will be influenced by two factors: the type of classroom setup and the particular methods and styles employed by each of your teachers.

Each of the following general class formats will require you to make adjustments to accomplish your goals.

Pure lectures are quite common from the college level up, but exist only rarely at the high school level. Some of the more popular courses (or introductory classes) at large colleges may attract hundreds of students.

Skills emphasized: listening; note-taking.

Also called *tutorials* and *seminars, discussion groups* are again common on the college level, often as adjuncts to courses boasting particularly large enrollments. A typical weekly schedule for such a course might consist of two lectures and one or more discussion groups. Often led by graduate teaching assistants (TAs), these discussion groups contain fewer students—often a dozen or fewer—and give you the chance to discuss points made in the lecture and material from assigned readings.

Such groups don't necessarily follow a precise text or format and may wander wildly from topic to topic, once again pointing out the need for a general mastery of the course material, the "jumping off" point for discussion.

Skills emphasized: asking/answering questions; analyzing concepts and ideas; taking part in discussion.

Some post-secondary courses are, for want of a better term, *combination classes*—they combine the lecture and discussion formats (the kind of pre-college class you're probably used to). The teacher prepares a lesson plan of the material he or she wants to cover in a specific class through lecture, discussion, question and answer, audio-visual presentation, or a combination of one or more such devices.

Your preparation for this type of class will depend to a great extent on the approach of the individual instructor. Such classes also occur on the post-secondary level—college, graduate school, trade school—when class size is too small for a formal lecture approach.

Skills emphasized: note-taking; listening; participation; asking and answering questions.

Hands-on classes such as science labs and various vocational education courses (industrial arts, graphics, and so forth) occur at all levels from middle school up. They are concerned almost exclusively with *doing* something—completing a particular experiment, working on a project, making a bookcase. The teacher may demonstrate certain things before letting the students work on their own, but the primary emphasis is on the student carrying out his or her own projects while in class.

On the college level, science labs are usually overseen by graduate assistants. Trade schools may use a combination of short lectures, demonstrations, and hands-on workshops; you can't become a good auto mechanic just by reading a book on cleaning a distributor.

Skills emphasized: development and application of particular manual, mechanical, or scientific techniques.

While some classes can't be neatly pigeonholed into one of these formats, most will be primarily one or another. It would seem that size is a key factor in choosing a format, but you can't always assume that a large course of 200 or more students will feature a professor standing behind a rostrum reading from his prepared text. Or that a small class of a dozen people will tend to be all discussion.

During my college years, I had a Religion teacher who, though his class was one of the more popular on campus and regularly drew 300 or more students to each session, rarely lectured at all. I never knew *what* to expect when entering his classroom. One class would feature a series of musical improvisations by a local jazz band, with a variety of graduate assistants talking about out-of-body experiences. Another session featured the professor arguing for nearly an hour with a single student about an idea or concept that had absolutely *nothing* to do with that week's (or any *other* week's) assignment.

In another class of merely 20 students, the professor teaching us Physical Chemistry would march in at the sound of the bell and, without acknowledging anyone's presence or saying a word, walk to the blackboard and start writing equations. He would wordlessly work his way across the massive board, until, some 20 or 30 minutes later, he ran off the right side. Slowly, he would walk back to the left side...and start erasing and writing all over again. He never asked questions or asked *for* them. In fact, I'm not sure I remember him uttering *any*thing for three solid months!

Thriving in a virtual classroom

For many of you, the term "classroom" may be virtually nonexistent (literally); yours may be wherever you can access Wi-Fi.

"Long distance learning" used to mean mail order correspondence courses, which evolved into packages of taped lectures, then relatively crude reproductions of presentations on CD and DVD. Not that long ago, there were only a handful of reputable online colleges like the University of Phoenix and Berkeley College amid a crazy quilt of dubious course offerings and downright fraudulent diploma mills.

In the last decade, the spread of computers and the evolution of the Internet radically changed the nature and availability of long-distance learning options. Today hundreds of major universities, from Stanford and UCLA to the bastions of the Ivy League, allow you to take classes and, in some cases, even earn advanced degrees without ever stepping foot on campus, meeting a professor face-to-face, or attending a single class in person.

Virtual classes can be any size—Massive Open Online Courses (MOOCs), for instance, can be, well, massive.

They can require all students to participate at the same time or let them access the material any time they wish.

They can mimic traditional courses—with designated dates and meeting times—or let you start and stop any lesson (or the entire course) whenever you wish, completing it in a few weeks or a few months.

I am in favor of any development that gives students greater and easier access to education. If such virtual courses—even an entire degree-granting curriculum—are the best or only way for you to reach your educational goals, I encourage you to take advantage of them. I would only caution you to make sure you have the discipline necessary to succeed in such a self-directed environment.

As far as I am concerned, the particular format of the classroom, even if it's a virtual one, does not affect the skills you need to use in it.

Know your teacher

You should also take the time to identify the *kind* of teacher you have, including an analysis of his or her likes, dislikes, preferences, style, and expectations. Depending on your "profile" of each teacher's habits, goals, and tendencies, preparation may vary quite a bit, whatever the topic or format of the class.

Consider something as simple as asking questions during class, which I encourage you to do whenever you don't understand a key point. Some teachers are very confident fielding questions at any time during a lesson; others prefer that questions be held until the end of the day's lesson; still others discourage questions (or any interaction for that matter) entirely. Learn when and how each one of your teachers likes to answer questions, then ask them accordingly.

No matter how ready a class is to enter into a free-wheeling discussion, some teachers fear losing control if they venture too far from their very specific lesson plans. Such teachers may well encourage discussion but always try to steer it into a predetermined path (their lesson plan). Other teachers thrive on chaos, in which case you can never be sure what's going to happen.

Approaching a class with the former teacher should lead you to participate as much as possible in the class discussion, but warn you to stay within whatever boundaries she has obviously set.

Getting ready for a class taught by the latter kind of teacher requires much more than just reading the text—there will be a lot of emphasis on your understanding key concepts, interpretation, analysis, and your ability to apply those lessons to situations or problems never mentioned in your text at all!

Some teachers' lesson plans or lectures are, at worst, a review of what's in the text and, at best, a review plus some discussion of sticky points or areas they feel may give you problems. Others use the text or other assignments merely as a jumping-off point—their lectures or lesson plans might cover numerous points that aren't in your text at all. Preparing for the latter kind of class will require much more than rote memorization of facts and figures—you'll have to be ready to give examples, explain concepts in context, and more.

Most of your teachers and professors will probably have the same goals: to teach you how to think, learn important facts and principles of the specific subject they teach, and, perhaps, how to apply them in your own way.

In math or science classes, your ability to apply what you've learned to specific problems is paramount.

Other classes, such as English, will require you to analyze and interpret various works, but may emphasize the "correct" interpretation, too.

Whatever situation you find yourself in—and you may well have one or more of each of these "types"—you will need to adapt the skills we cover in this chapter to each.

And learn her style

All effective instructors develop a plan of attack for each class. They decide which points they will make, how much time they will spend reviewing assignments and previous lessons, what texts they will refer to, and how much time they will allow for questions.

Building a note-taking strategy around each teacher's typical "plan of attack" for lectures is another key to academic success. Why do some students just seem to know what's important and what's not? How do they ferret out exactly the information that's "test-worthy" while not even glancing at the material that isn't?

What these students innately know is that items discussed during *any* lesson can be grouped into four distinct categories:

> ❯ Information not contained in the class text(s) or other assigned reading.
> ❯ Explanations of obscure material covered in the text but with which students may have difficulty.
> ❯ Demonstrations or examples to further explain a concept, process, or subject.
> ❯ Background information to put course material in context.

As you listen to your teacher, try to figure out which category his remarks fall into. This will help you determine how extensive and detailed your notes on that segment of the lecture should be.

Teachers are only human and therefore *can* be impressed by small gestures. Without adopting *too* obsequious an attitude, staying after class occasionally or stopping by during a professor's office hours are simple ways to make a good impression. And if your teacher offers any assignments for extra credit—more usual at the high school level than college—do them! Even less than superior work may still earn you a couple of extra points.

How to prepare for any class

In general, here's how to prepare for any class before you walk through the door (or power up your computer) and take your seat.

Read the syllabus

...and any other course information handed out the first day of class or posted online.

A typical syllabus for a college class may include:

> Course number, location and schedule
> Instructor (name, phone, email, office hours)
> Required texts and materials
> Supplemental (optional) texts and materials
> Official course description, including prerequisites
> Learning objectives
> Code of conduct, including attendance, cell-phone, and other policies
> Details of class operation
> Grading structure, including how exams, reports, and class participation will be weighted

Professors will assume that students have the good sense to carefully review all of the requirements and policies included in a syllabus and may never go over them in class. Your explanations of why you failed to follow detailed formatting instructions for a report or presentation or forgot when the second quiz was scheduled will not be welcomed or accepted.

Complete all assignments

Regardless of a particular teacher's style or the classroom format he is using, virtually every course you take will have a formal text (or two or three or more) assigned to it. Though the way the text explains or covers particular topics may differ substantially from your teacher's approach to the same material, your text is still the basis of the course and a key ingredient in your studying. You *must* read it, plus any other assigned books, *before* you get to class.

You may sometimes feel you can get away without reading assigned books beforehand, especially in a lecture format where you *know* the chance of being called on is between slim and none. But fear of being questioned on it is certainly not the only reason I stress reading the material that's been assigned. You will be lost if the professor decides—for the first time ever!—to spend the entire period asking the students questions. I've had it happen. And it is *not* a pleasant experience for the unprepared.

You'll find it harder to take clear and concise notes in class when you can't differentiate new material from what's in the text—in which case you will be frantically copying down material you could have underlined in your book the night before. You'll also find it difficult to evaluate the relative importance of the teacher's remarks.

If you're heading for a discussion group, how can you participate without your reading as a basis? I think the scariest feeling in the world is sitting in a classroom knowing that, sooner or later, you are going to be called on, and you don't know the material.

Remember: Completing your reading assignment means not just reading the *main* text but any *other* books, articles, or handouts assigned. It also means completing any non-reading assignments—turning in a lab report, preparing a list of topics, or being ready to present your oral report.

Needless to say, while doing your homework is important, *turning it in* is an essential second step! My daughter,

Lindsay, refused to use any organizational system when she was in elementary school. As a result, she either forgot to pack the homework she had done or left it in her backpack and failed to turn it in.

My solution was to give her a bright red manila folder, marked "HOMEWORK," into which she deposited every assignment as soon as she finished it. And she had to place the folder on top of her backpack, where it couldn't be forgotten, before she went to bed. Before every class, she pulled out the folder to see if she had something to turn in.

Sometimes the simplest solutions are the most effective.

Review your notes

Your teacher is probably going to start this lecture or discussion from the point she left off last time. And you probably won't remember where that was unless you check your notes.

Prepare your questions

This is your chance to find the answers to the questions that are still puzzling you. Review your questions before class. That way, you'll be able to check off the ones the teacher answers along the way and only need to ask those left unanswered.

Prepare your attitude

Don't discount the importance of the way you approach each class mentally. Getting the most out of school in general and any class in particular depends to some extent on how ready you are to wholeheartedly participate in the process. It is *not* sufficient, even if you are otherwise well-prepared, to just sit back and absorb the information. Learning requires your active participation every step of the way.

What to do in class

Keep in mind your own preferences and under what circumstances you do best—refer back to the first two chapters and review your skills lists. Concentrate on the courses that have historically given you the most trouble.

Sit right up front

Although you may still choose not to, I do have to recommend that you minimize distractions by sitting as close to the instructor as you can.

The farther you sit from the teacher, the more difficult it is to listen. Sitting toward the back of the room means more heads bobbing around in front of you and more students staring out the window or at their cellphones, encouraging you to do the same.

Sitting up front has several benefits. You will make a terrific first impression on the instructor—you might well be the only student sitting in the front row. He'll see immediately that you have come to class to listen and learn, not just take up space.

You'll be able to hear the instructor without straining, and the instructor will be able to hear *you* when you ask or answer questions.

Finally, being able to see the teacher clearly will help ensure that your eyes don't wander around the room and out the window, taking your brain with them.

Fortunately or unfortunately, following this advice will make it much more difficult for you to surreptitiously slip out the back door before class ends.

Avoid distracting classmates

Your classmates may be wonderful friends, entertaining lunch companions, and delightful dorm mates, but their quirks, idiosyncrasies, and personal hygiene habits can prove distracting when you sit next to them in class.

Knuckle-cracking, giggling, whispering, and note-passing are just some of the evils that can divert your attention in the middle of your math teacher's discourse on Euclid. Avoid them.

Listen for verbal clues

Identifying noteworthy material means separating the wheat—that which you *should* write down—from the chaff—that which you should *ignore*. Do that by *listening* for verbal clues and *watching* for the nonverbal ones.

Certainly not all teachers will give you the clues you're seeking. But many will invariably signal important material in the way they present it—pausing; repeating a point (perhaps one already made in your textbook); slowing down their normally supersonic lecture speed; speaking more loudly (or softly); or stating, "I think the following is important" or, even better, "This will be on the test."

There are also numerous words and phrases that should *signal* noteworthy material (and, at the same time, give you the clues you need to logically organize your notes): "First of all," "Most importantly," "Therefore," "As a result," "To summarize," "On the other hand," "On the contrary," "The following (number of) reasons (or causes, effects, decisions, facts, and so on)."

Such words and phrases give you the clues to not just write down the material that follows, but also to put it in context—to make a list ("First," "The following reasons"); establish a cause-and-effect relationship ("Therefore," "As a result"); identify opposites or alternatives ("On the other hand," "On the contrary"); signify a conclusion ("Therefore," "To summarize"); or offer an explanation or definition.

Watch for nonverbal clues

Studies have shown that only a fraction of communication is conveyed by words alone. A great deal of the message we receive when someone is speaking to us comes from body language, facial expression, and tone of voice.

Most instructors will go off on tangents of varying relevance to the subject matter. Some of these digressions will be important, but, at least during your first few lessons with that particular teacher, you won't know which.

Body language can be your clue. If the teacher begins looking at the window or his eyes glaze over, he's sending a clear signal: "This won't be on any test."

On the other hand, if he makes eye contact with several students while gesturing dramatically, he's sending a very obvious signal about the importance of the point he's making.

Ask questions

No, don't raise your hand to ask or answer questions every 90 seconds. Being an active listener means asking *yourself* if you understand everything that has been discussed. If you don't, ask the instructor questions at an appropriate time or write down the questions you need answered to fully understand the subject.

Challenge yourself to draw conclusions from what the instructor is saying. Think about the subject matter and how it relates to what you've been assigned to read and other facts to which you've been exposed.

Take clear, concise notes

I'm sure you've observed in your classes that some people are constantly taking notes. Others end up with two lines on one page. Most of us fall in between.

The person who never stops taking notes is either writing a letter to a friend in Iowa or has absolutely no idea what *is* or is *not* important. To use that old adage, she can't see the forest for the trees. She probably also underlines or highlights every other word in her textbook.

Her opposite number barely takes notes at all. He may perk up when the teacher says, "Now, write this down and remember it," but is otherwise near comatose.

Watch him sweat when it's time to study for the exam. Without good class notes, he will be left frantically thumbing through a textbook that contains a fraction of what he needs to know for the test.

Taking concise, clear notes is, first and foremost, the practice of discrimination—developing your ability to separate the essential from the superfluous, to identify and retain key concepts, facts, and ideas and ignore the rest. In turn, this requires the ability to listen to what your teacher is saying and write down only what you need to understand the concept. For some, that could mean a single sentence. For others, a detailed example will suffice.

Just remember: The quality of your notes usually has little to do with their *length*—three key lines that reveal the core concepts of a whole lecture are far more valuable than paragraphs of less important data.

Even if you find yourself wandering helplessly in the lecturer's wake, so unsure of what she's saying that you can't begin to separate the important, noteworthy material from the nonessential verbiage, use the techniques discussed in this chapter to organize and condense your notes anyway.

Many teachers are now posting their own notes (and the PowerPoint slides from their lectures) online to save students time and anguish.

But learn to be selective

You *know* the capital of Great Britain. You *know* the chemical formula for water. And you *know* Ernest Hemingway wrote *The Old Man and the Sea*. So why waste time and space writing them down?

Your teachers may present material you already know in order to set the stage for further discussion or to introduce material that is more difficult. Don't be so conditioned to copy dates, vocabulary, terms, formulas, and names that you mindlessly scribble down information you already know. You'll just be wasting your time—both in class and later, when you review your overly detailed notes.

This is why some experts recommend that you bring your notes or outline of your textbook reading to class and then *add your class notes to them.*

Just remember, taking effective notes requires five separate actions on your part:

> ❯ *Listening* actively
> ❯ *Selecting* pertinent information
> ❯ *Condensing* it
> ❯ *Sorting*/organizing it
> ❯ *Interpreting* it (later)

Develop your shorthand skills

You don't have to be a master of shorthand to streamline your note-taking. Here are five ways:

1. Eliminate vowels. As a sign that was ubiquitous in the New York City subways used to proclaim, "If u cn rd ths, u cn gt a gd jb." ("If you can read this, you can get a good job.") And, we might add, "u cn b a btr stdnt."

2. Use word beginnings ("rep" for representative, "Dem" for Democrat) and other easy-to-remember abbreviations.

3. Stop putting periods after all abbreviations. (They add up!)

4. Use standard symbols in place of words. The following list, some of which you may recognize from math or logic courses, may help you:

≈	approximately
w/	with
w/o	without
wh/	which
→	resulting in
←	as a result of/consequence of
+	and or also
*	most importantly
cf	compare; in comparison; in relation to
ff	following
<	less than
>	more than
=	the same as
↑	increasing
↓	decreasing
esp	especially
Δ	change
⊂	it follows that
∴	therefore
b/c	because

5. Create your own symbols and abbreviations based on your needs and comfort-level.

There are three specific symbols I think you'll want to create—they'll be needed again and again:

(W) That's my symbol for "*What?*" as in "What the heck does that mean?" "What did she say?" or "What happened? I'm completely lost!" It denotes something that's been missed; leave space in your notes to fill in the missing part of the puzzle after class.

(M) That's my symbol for "My idea" or "My thought." I want to separate my thoughts during a lecture from the professor's

(T) My symbol for "Test!" as in "This information will definitely be on the test, so don't forget to review it!!!"

You may want to create specific symbols or abbreviations for each class. In chemistry, "TD" may stand for thermodynamics, "K" for the Kinetic Theory of Gases (but don't mix it up with the "K" for Kelvin), and "BL" for Boyle's Law. In history, "GW" is the Father of our country, "ABE" is Mr. Honesty, and "FR" is the French Revolution.

How do you keep everything straight? Create a list on the first page of each class's notebook (or in an online file) of the abbreviations and symbols you intend to use regularly through the semester.

Just be careful—in your fervor to adopt my shorthand system, don't abbreviate so much that your notes are absolutely unintelligible to you almost as soon as you write them!

You may choose to abbreviate a little less and write a little more. Whatever system you adopt, just make sure it serves its purpose: giving you the time to *listen* to your instructors rather than just furiously copying everything they say.

The Cornell System

This is a well-known note-taking system many college students are taught. If it works for you, use it.

Start by drawing a vertical line two to three inches from the left side of a piece of paper. Take notes to the *right* of this line.

During the lecture: Take notes as you normally would—in paragraph form, outline, or using your own shorthand.

After the lecture: Reread your notes and reduce them to the key words that will help you recall the important points of the lecture. Write those key words and phrases in the *left*-hand column.

As you master this technique, you will find that reviewing for a test will only require studying the left-hand column—short and concise—not the right.

It should be no problem adapting this method if you prefer taking lecture notes on your laptop or tablet.

Actively participate in every class

In many non-lecture classes, you will find that discussion, mostly in the form of questions and answers, is actively encouraged. This dialogue serves to both confirm your knowledge and comprehension of specific subject matter and to identify those areas in which you need work.

Participate in any discussion to the best of your ability. Most teachers consider class participation a key ingredient in your semester grades. No matter how many papers and tests you ace, if you never open your mouth in class, you shouldn't be surprised to get less than an A.

If you're having trouble following an argument or particular line of thought, ask for a review or for clarification. Based on the professor's preferences and the class format, ask the questions you feel need answers.

Be careful you don't innocently distract yourself from practicing your now-excellent note-taking skills by starting to analyze something you don't understand or, worse, creating mental arguments because you disagree with something your teacher or a classmate said. Taking the time to mentally frame an elaborate question is equally distracting. All three behaviors lead to the same problem: *You're not listening!*

Finally, listen closely to the words of your classmates—you'll often find their comments, attitudes, and opinions as helpful and insightful as your instructor's.

What if you're shy or just get numb whenever you're called on? Ask a question rather than taking part in the discussion—it's easier and, over time, may help you break the ice and jump into the discussion. If you really can't open your mouth without running a fever, consider taking a public speaking course.

Most importantly, prepare and practice. Fear of standing in front of a class or even participating from the safety of your seat is, for many of you, just a symptom of lack of confidence.

And lack of confidence stems from lack of preparation. The more prepared you are—if you know the material backward and forward—the more likely you will be able to, even *want* to, raise your hand and "strut your stuff." Practicing with friends, parents, or relatives may also help.

If you are having trouble with oral reports, they are covered separately in Chapter 8. I think you'll find the hints I've included there will eliminate a lot of the fear such talks seem to engender.

What to do *after* class

As soon as possible after your class, review your notes, fill in the "blanks," mark down questions you need to research in your text or ask during the next class, and add any new assignments to your calendar.

I tend to discourage recopying your notes as a general practice, since I believe it's more important to work on taking good notes in the first place and not wasting the time it takes to recopy them. But if you tend to write fast and illegibly, it may make sense to rewrite your notes so they're readable, taking the opportunity to summarize as you go. The better your notes, the better your chance of capturing and recalling the pertinent material.

It may not be easy for most high school students to do so, but in college, where you are given more autonomy in scheduling your classes, I recommend "one period on, one off"—an open period, even a half hour, after each class to review that class's notes and prepare for the next one.

If you find yourself unable to take advantage of such in-between time, schedule as little time between classes as you can.

What if you missed class?

Even if you diligently apply all of the tips in this chapter, they will all be useless if you regularly miss class. So don't! It is especially important to attend all classes near the end of each quarter or semester. Teachers sometimes use the last week of class to review the entire semester's work (what a great way to minimize your own review time), clarify topics they feel might still be fuzzy, and/or answer questions. Students invariably ask about the final exam during this period, and some teachers may reveal some particulars about what's going to be on the test.

If you must miss a class, find the best note taker and ask to borrow *his* notes. Some professors might let you borrow their own notes or post them online.

Chapter 7

Ready your Research

"Knowledge is of two kinds: we know a subject ourselves,
or we know where we can find information upon it."

—Samuel Johnson

In high school or college, you will have to prepare written and/or oral reports for virtually every one of your non-science classes (and lab reports for the others).

In this chapter, I'll cover general rules you need to follow for any paper or report, advice on how to conduct research at the library or online, and all the other steps you need to complete before actually writing a single word of your paper.

In Chapter 8, we will cover everything necessary to transform your detailed research into a well-written, well-presented term paper or oral report.

Reading these two chapters will not make you such a good writer that you can quit school and start visiting bookstores to preen in front of the window displays featuring your latest bestseller.

But there is absolutely no reason to fear a written paper or oral report, once you know the simple steps to take and rules to follow to complete it satisfactorily. Once you realize that 90 percent of preparing a paper has *nothing* to do with writing... or even being *able* to write. And once you're confident that preparing papers by following my suggestions will probably get you a grade or two higher than you've gotten before...even if you think you are the world's poorest excuse for a writer.

Doing a research paper requires a lot of work. But the payoff is great, too. You will learn, for example:

> How to track down information about *any* subject.
> How to sort through that information and come to a conclusion about your subject.
> How to prepare an organized, in-depth report.
> How to communicate your ideas clearly and effectively.

Of all the things you'll learn in school, the skills you acquire as you produce your research paper will be among the most valuable.

Once you develop these skills, you'll be able to apply them in *all* your high school or college classes, not only when you prepare other research papers, but also when you tackle smaller assignments, such as essays, book reports, or lab reports.

When you graduate, these same skills will help you get ahead in the work world; the ability to analyze a subject and write about it in clear, concise language will prove a highly valuable skill, no matter what career you choose.

Five fundamental rules

Let's start with the fundamental rules that need to be emblazoned on your mind:

> *Always* follow your teacher's directions to the letter.
> *Always* hand in your paper on time.
> *Always* hand in a clean and clear copy of your paper.
> *Always* keep at least one copy of every paper you write.
> *Never* allow a spelling or grammatical error in any paper you prepare.

You wanted it type*written?*

Your teacher's directions may include:

> A general subject area from which topics should be chosen—"some aspect of Woodrow Wilson's presidency," "a Supreme Court decision," "a short story by Edgar Allen Poe," or "one of Isaac Newton's Laws."
> Specific requirements regarding format.
> Suggested length.
> Preferred methods for including footnotes or endnotes and documenting works consulted or cited.
> Other specific instructions.

Whatever his or her directions, *follow them to the letter.* Some high school teachers may forgive you your trespasses, but I have known college professors who simply refused to accept a paper that was not prepared *exactly* as they instructed—and gave the poor but wiser student an F (without even *reading* it).

At some point, you'll undoubtedly run into a teacher or professor who gives few or no instructions at all. You ask, "How long should the paper be?" She says, "As long as it takes." Use your common sense. If you're in middle or high school, I doubt she is seeking a 50-page thesis. But your college professor probably won't consider three pages—with *really* wide margins—an acceptable length for any paper. Use previous assignments as a guide.

If you are unsure of a specific requirement or if the suggested area of topics is unclear, it is *your* responsibility to talk to your teacher and clarify whatever points are confusing you.

It is also not a bad idea to choose two or three topics you'd like to write about and seek preliminary approval if the assignment seems particularly vague.

There are no acceptable excuses

There is certainly no reason, short of catastrophic illness or life-threatening emergency, for you to *ever* be late with an assignment. Again, some teachers will refuse to accept a paper that is late. At best, they will mark you down for your lateness, perhaps turning an A into a B...or worse. In the case of extenuating circumstances (for example, extended illness, death in the family, and so on), notify your teacher immediately and arrange for an extension.

Presentation does matter

Teachers have to read a lot of papers and shouldn't be faulted if, after hundreds of pages, they come upon your wrinkled, coffee-stained, pencil-written report and get a bit discouraged.

Nor should you be surprised if they give you a lower grade than the content might merit *just because the presentation was so poor.*

Granted, the content is what the teacher is looking for, and he *should* be grading you on *what* you write. But presentation *is* important. You can't fault a teacher for trying to teach you to take pride in your work. So follow these suggestions:

> Never handwrite your paper.
> Whether typewritten or printed, make sure all pages are crisp and clear.
> Unless otherwise instructed, always double space your paper. And leave adequate (but not excessive) margins all around.
> Use a simple typeface that is clear and easy-to-read; avoid those that are too big—stretching a five-page paper to ten—or too small and hard to read.
> Never use a fancy italic, gothic, modern, or other ornate or hard-to-read typeface for the entire paper.

What can your old papers teach you?

There should be a number of helpful comments in your returned papers, which is why it's so important to retain them. What did your teacher have to say? Are her comments applicable to the paper you're writing now—poor grammar, lack of organization, lack of research, bad transitions between paragraphs, misspellings? The more such comments—and, one would expect, the lower the grade—the more extensive the "map" your teacher has given you for your *next* paper, showing you the exact spot to "locate" your A+.

If you got a low grade on a previous paper but there weren't any comments, ask the teacher why you got such a poor grade. You may get the comments you need to make the next paper better *and* show the teacher you actually care, which could also help your grade the next time around.

Many employers merrily use resumes and cover letters with grammatical and/or spelling errors for wastebasket hoops practice. Don't expect your teachers to be any more forgiving—there are definitely a few out there who will award an F without even noticing that the rest of the paper is great. Guess it's just too bad you misspelled "Constantinople" or left a participle dangling slowly in the wind.

How to conduct your research

Start any research project by working with the broadest outlines or topics (and the broadest resources) and slowly narrow your focus, getting more and more specific in topic and sources as you go along.

Encyclopedic entries are usually the most comprehensive and concise you will find. They cover so much territory and are so (relatively) up to date that they are an ideal "big picture" resource. (Just remember they are only your starting point. Most teachers will not accept papers that exclusively paraphrase *Wikipedia*; nor will they deem acceptable a bibliography consisting entirely of three encyclopedias or a list of websites of dubious heritage.)

Consider moving next to a subject-specific encyclopedia. There is seemingly a tome on anything you can think of, to wit: *Encyclopedia of Christmas, Charlie Chan Film Encyclopedia, Encyclopedia of Paleontology, Encyclopedia of the Renaissance, Encyclopedia of Deserts, Encyclopedia of Smoking and Tobacco, Historical Encyclopedia of Nursing,* and the *Oxford Companion to Food.*

If you are writing a paper about a historical or contemporary figure, consider skimming a biographical dictionary or one of the specific volumes in the *Who's Who* series, which ranges from *Who's Who in Art* and *Who's Who in American Jewry* to *Who's Who in Theatre* and *Who's Who in Vietnam*.

New reference websites, of course, appear almost hourly. These many current resources should make it increasingly easy to choose a good topic, establish a reasonable thesis, and gather enough information to construct an initial outline, without having to do any further research.

But completing an A+ paper will still require you to turn to other sources for more detailed information. You need to read books written by experts in the field you're researching, as well as magazine, newspaper, and journal articles about every aspect of your subject.

Why stop there? Pamphlets, anthologies, brochures, government documents, films, and videos are just some other possible sources of information for your paper.

Evaluating resources

You may find so many potential resources that you won't have time to read them all. Concentrate on those that have been published most recently or written by the most respected sources. However, don't limit yourself *too* much—gather information from a wide range of sources. Otherwise, you may learn only one side of the story.

There are two types of resources: *primary* and *secondary*.

Primary resources are those written by people who *actually witnessed or participated in an event*. When you read a scientist's report about an experiment she has conducted, you are consulting a primary resource.

Secondary resources are those written by people *who were not actually present at an event,* but have studied the subject. When you read a book about the 1950s written by someone who was born in 1960, you are learning from a secondary resource.

Primary resources are likely to be more reliable sources of information. But depending upon your subject, there may not be any primary resources available to you.

Where to look for materials

How do you find out whether anyone has written a magazine or newspaper article about your topic? How do you know if there are any government documents or pamphlets that might be of help? How do you locate those written-by-the-experts reference books?

You either go to your local public or school library and consult its publication indexes, which list all of the articles, books, and other materials that have been published and/or are available in your library, or you go online.

How libraries are organized

Many libraries have been at the forefront of adapting technology to make their collections more accessible. The card catalog, once actually kept on index cards but now most likely computerized, indexes available books by subject, author, and title. And a wide variety of databases, programs, and apps have replaced the newspaper microfiches, vertical files, even many of the multi-volume encyclopedias that populated the Reference Room. Check with your local public, school, or college librarian to familiarize yourself with the particular ins-and-outs of your library.

To provide organization and facilitate access, most small and academic libraries utilize the Dewey Decimal

Classification System, which uses numbers from 000 to 999 to classify all material by subject matter. It begins by organizing all books into 10 major groupings:

000–099	General
100–199	Philosophy
200–299	Religion
300–399	Social Sciences
400–499	Language
500–599	Natural Science and Mathematics
600–699	Technology
700–799	Fine Arts
800–899	Literature
900–999	General Geography and History

Given the millions of books available in major libraries, just dividing them into these 10 groups would still make it quite difficult to find a specific title. So each of the 10 major groupings is further divided into 10, and each of these now 100 groups is assigned to more specific subjects within each large group. For example, within the Philosophy classification (100), 150 is psychology and 170 is ethics. Within the History classification (900), 910 is travel and 930 is ancient history.

There is even further subdivision. Mathematics is given its own number in the 500 (Science) series—510. But specific subjects within mathematics are further classified: 511 is arithmetic, 512 is algebra, and so on.

Finally, the last two digits in the Dewey Decimal code signify the type of book:

01	Philosophy of
02	Outlines of
03	Dictionary of
04	Essays about

05 Periodicals on
06 Society transactions and proceedings
07 Study or teaching of
08 Collections
09 History of

If your library doesn't use the Dewey system, it probably is organized according to the Library of Congress System, which uses letters instead of numbers to denote major categories:

A General works (encyclopedias and other reference)
B Philosophy, Psychology, and Religion
C History: Auxiliary sciences (archeology, genealogy, and so on)
D History: General, non-American
E American history (general)
F American history (local)
G Geography/Anthropology
H Social sciences (sociology, business, economics)
J Political sciences
K Law
L Education
M Music
N Fine arts (art and architecture)
P Language/Literature
Q Sciences
R Medicine
S Agriculture
T Technology
U Military science
V Naval science
Z Bibliography/Library science

Online research

There's so much material on the Internet, it's easy to be over-whelmed. While it can be extremely helpful to have access to some obscure websites that have just the material you need, especially when a book or two you want to consult has disap-peared from the library, I am still convinced that most of you will waste too much time if the majority of your research is done online. It is ridiculously easy to get sidetracked when doing research online. "Wow, I didn't know there were that many cool sites about Matthew McConaughey. I'd better check them all out...right now!"

While much of the "basic" information on most research-oriented websites is not going to radically change from day to day, that is certainly not true of all sites. Just as the identical keyword search may yield radically different results if run on two separate days (or two different search engines), you may find material you need deleted the next time you look for it. So if you find something really good, download it, save it to your hard drive, or print a hard copy.

Amazon and other online bookstores will list many books before they are published, and almost always before your local library has ordered, cataloged, and shelved them (or an E-book version is available). Many of these sites now feature searchable pages of many titles—from a table of contents and short excerpt to 50 pages of text or more. This should help you get a feel for whether the book or a portion of it is pertinent to your topic.

Amazon in particular offers a "People who bought this book also bought" feature, which is a good way to locate related resources.

There's no room in this book to list even a smattering of pertinent Internet sites. Wherever you go online, just remember:

> ❯ Some of the sites are informative and well-organized; some are quirky and skimpy.

> ❯ Some are well-researched and trustworthy; some are the rantings of a mad person. Just because something is on your computer screen doesn't mean it's true.

> ❯ Some provide unbiased information with no ulterior motive; some slant their information to sell you on their cause. Some are offering information just to entice you to buy something.

> ❯ Some are easy to use; some require you to search through listings to find what you need.

> ❯ Some supply information; some link you to other sites; some are simply listings of sites.

> ❯ Some may be gone when you look for them again.

> ❯ Some are free; some cost a bit...some cost a lot. Be sure to check out the cost before using a site where you have to pay.

Despite the immensity and importance of the Internet's resources, brick-and-mortar libraries are certainly not dinosaurs. Just because you can visit nearly any library in the world without leaving your computer screen is no reason to avoid becoming intimately familiar with your local or school library. You will find that doing *some* things online is not always as interesting, efficient, or fun as doing them in person.

The Fry paper-writing system

Now let's look at all the steps necessary to create a terrific paper, report, presentation, or speech for any class.

The more complex a task or the longer you need to complete it, the more important your organization becomes.

By breaking down any project into a series of manageable steps, you'll immediately start to feel less chaotic, hectic, and afraid.

Here are the steps that, with some minor variations along the way, are common to virtually any written report or paper:

1. Research potential topics.
2. Finalize topic.
3. Begin your initial research.
4. Create general outline.
5. Do detailed research.
6. Prepare a detailed outline (from note cards).
7. Write the first draft.
8. Do additional research (if necessary).
9. Write the second draft (and keep rewriting).
10. Prepare your final bibliography.
11. Check spelling and grammar.
12. Have someone *else* proofread.
13. Produce final draft.
14. Proofread one last time.
15. Turn it in and collect your A+.

Create a work schedule

Doing all these tasks efficiently and effectively requires careful timing and planning. This may not be the only assignment—or even the only paper—you have to finish in a short amount of time.

So get out your calendar and mark the date your paper is due. How many weeks till then? Four? Six? Ten? Plan to spend from one-half to three-quarters of your time on research, the rest on writing.

Block out set periods of time during each week to work on your paper. Try to schedule large chunks of time—at least two or three hours, if possible—rather than many short periods. Otherwise, you'll spend too much time trying to remember where you left off and repeat steps unnecessarily.

As you make up your work schedule, set deadlines for completing various steps of your paper. Plan on consulting and/or taking notes from at least six different sources. (Your teacher or subject may require more; I doubt you will need fewer.) And plan on producing at least two or three drafts of your paper before you consider it final.

Refer to your work schedule often, and adjust your pace if you find yourself lagging behind.

Steps 1 & 2: Research and finalize your topic

In some cases, your teacher will assign your topic. In others, he will assign a general area of study, but you will have the freedom to pick a specific topic.

There are some pitfalls you should avoid. Let's say you need to write a 12-page paper for your government class, and you decide your topic will be "Disability-Related Legislation in American History." Can you really cover a topic that broad in a dozen pages? No, you can't. You could write volumes on the subject (people have!) and have plenty left to say.

Instead, you need to focus on a particular, limited aspect of such a broad subject, such as, "The Passage of the ADA (Americans With Disabilities Act)." That would probably work for a middle or high school paper. After your initial research, you may decide even *that* topic is too broad, in which case you would further narrow your scope.

Choose a subject that's too *limited*, and you might run out of things to say on the second page of your paper. "The Chapman Amendment of the ADA" might make an interesting three- or four-page essay, but you won't fill 10 or 15 pages...even with a 14-point font and really wide margins.

Make sure there is enough research material available about your topic. And make sure that there are enough *different* sources of material so you can get a well-rounded view of your subject (and not be forced for lack of other material to find ways to make somebody else's points sound like your own).

Pick a topic that's too obscure, and you may find that little or no information has been written about it at all. In that case, you will have to conduct your own experiments, interview your own research subjects, and come up with your own original data. I'm guessing that you have neither the time, desire, nor experience to take such an approach.

Taking all of the above into consideration, do a little brainstorming now about possible topics for your paper. Don't just settle for the first idea—come up with several different possibilities. Put this book down until you have a list of three or four potential topics.

How about trying to get papers for two or more classes *out of the same research?* You may not be able to simply produce one paper for two classes, but with a little extra research—*not* as much as you would need to do for an entirely different paper—you may well utilize a good portion of the first paper as the basis for a second. What a great way to maximize your research time!

Step 3: Begin your initial research

Got your list of potential topics? Then go to your library. You need to do a little advance research. Scan your library's card-catalog index and *Readers' Guide to Periodical Literature* or other publication indexes. See how many books and articles have been written about each topic on your "possibilities" list. Next, read a short background article or encyclopedia entry about each topic.

Alternatively, spend a little time online. Are there specific websites devoted to your topic? Or does a keyword search result in 104,424 matches, most of which have *nothing* to do with your topic?

With any luck at all, you should be left with at least one topic that looks like a good research subject. If two or more topics passed your preliminary-research test, pick the one that interests you most. You're going to spend a lot of time learning about your subject. There's no rule that says you can't enjoy it!

DEVELOP A TEMPORARY THESIS

Once you have chosen the topic for your paper, you must develop a temporary thesis. (The word "thesis" is a relative of "hypothesis" and means about the same thing—the central argument you will attempt to prove or disprove in your paper. A thesis is not the same thing as a *topic*. Your topic is what you study; your thesis is the conclusion you draw from that study.)

A "thesis statement" sums up the main point of your paper in just a sentence or two.

Note that I said *temporary* thesis. It may not wind up being your final thesis. Because you haven't completed all your research yet, you can only propose a "best-guess" thesis at this point.

If a temporary thesis doesn't spring easily to mind—and it probably won't—sit back and do some more brainstorming. Ask yourself questions like:

> ❯ What's special or unusual about ____? (Fill in the blank with your topic.)
> ❯ How is ____ related to events in the past?
> ❯ What impact has ____ made on society?
> ❯ What do I want the world to know about ____?
> ❯ What questions do I have about ____?

You may discover during this preliminary research phase that your temporary thesis just won't fly. You may have to revise it, perhaps even settling on a thesis that's the exact opposite of your original! In fact, you may have to revise your thesis several times during the course of your research.

Step 4: Create a general outline

Once you have developed your temporary thesis, think about how you might approach the subject in your paper. Jot down the various issues you plan to investigate. Then come up with a brief, temporary outline of your paper, showing the order in which you might discuss those issues.

Don't worry too much about this outline—it will be brief, at best. It's simply a starting point for your research, a plan of attack. But don't skip this step, either—it will be a big help in organizing your research findings.

Step 5: Do detailed research

We've already reviewed library and online resources and how to take advantage of them. Now, let's talk about exactly how you'll keep track of all the resources and information you'll gather for your paper.

There are two steps involved. First, you'll create bibliography cards for each source you want to review. Then, you'll transfer all the information from your bibliography cards to a single list—your working bibliography. This two-step method will help you conduct your research in an organized, efficient manner and simplify the preparation of your final bibliography.

To create your working bibliography, you'll need a supply of 3 x 5 index cards. You'll also use index cards when you take notes for your paper, so buy a big batch now. About 300 cards ought to suffice. While you're at it, pick up one of those little file boxes designed to hold the cards. Put your name, address, and phone number on the box. If you lose it, some kind stranger may (and hopefully will) return it.

Start a systematic search for any materials that might have information related to your paper. When you find a book, article, website or other resource that looks promising, take out a blank note card. On the front of the card, write down the following information:

In the upper right-hand corner of the card: Write the library call number (Dewey Decimal or Library of Congress number), if there is one, or the complete URL. Add any other details that will help you locate the material on the library shelves ("Science Reading Room," "Reference Room"). And make sure to write down the *complete* Web address.

On the main part of the card: Write the author's name, if given—last name first, followed by first name, then middle name or initial. Then the title of the article, if applicable, in quotation marks. Then the name of the book, magazine, newspaper, or other publication—underlined. (If you have already written the complete Internet address in the right-hand corner, you do not need to duplicate it here.)

Add any details you will need if you have to find the book or article again, such as the date of publication, edition, volume, and/or issue number, and page numbers on which the article or information appears.

In the upper left-hand corner of the card: Number it. The first card you write will be #1, the second, #2, and so on. If you happen to mess up and skip a number somewhere along the line, don't worry. It's only important that you assign a different number to each card.

Do this for *each* potential source of information you find, a*nd put only one resource on each card.* Leave some room on the card—you'll be adding more information later.

Sample Bibliography Card for a Book

1	315.6
	Main Reading Room

Spechler, Jay W.

Reasonable Accommodation: Profitable Compliance
with the Americans with Disabilities Act
(see esp. pp. 54–61)

Computer Card Catalog
College Library

Sample Bibliography Card for a Magazine Article

2   www.timeinc.com/pub/2003/index.html

Smolowe, Jill

"Noble Aims, Mixed Results"
Time
(July 31, 2003; pp. 54–55)

Sample Bibliography Card for a Newspaper Article

3   www.nytimes/index/404/5.html

Wade, Betsy

"Disabled Access to Inns at Issue"
The New York Times
(April 14, 2004, section 5, page 4)

CITING PRINT AND ONLINE INFORMATION

For guidelines on how to cite all your sources, consult the style manual from either the Modern Language Association (MLA) or American Psychological Association (APA). Your teacher has probably told you which she prefers. The *Chicago Manual of Style*, now in its 16th edition (2010), should also be consulted.

The MLA Handbook for Writers of Research Papers (for high school and undergraduate college students) is available in a seventh edition (2009). The third edition of *The MLA Style Manual and Guide to Scholarly Publishing* (for graduate students, scholars, and professional writers) was published in 2008. The sixth editions of *The Publication Manual of the APA* (2009) and *APA Style Guide to Electronic References* (2012) are the most current.

GET READY TO TAKE NOTES

Your bibliography cards serve as the map for your information treasure hunt. Get out a stack of five or six cards, and locate the materials listed on them. Set up camp at a secluded desk or table in the library or at home and get to work.

When you write your paper, you'll get all the information you need from your note cards, rather than from the original sources. Therefore, it's vital that you take careful and complete notes. What sort of information should you put on your note cards? Anything related to your subject and especially to your thesis. This includes:

> General background information (names, dates, historical data).
> Research statistics.
> Quotes by experts.
> Definitions of technical terms.

Before you fill out your first note card from any resource, recheck all of the information you entered on its bibliography card. Is the title exactly as printed? Is the author's name spelled correctly? Is there any information you need to include in your final bibliography?

NOTE-TAKING GUIDELINES

Once your bibliography card is finished, set it aside. Get out some blank index cards and start taking notes from your reference source. Follow these guidelines:

> **Write one thought, idea, quote, or fact on each card.** If you encounter a very long quote or string of data, you can write on both the front and back of a card, if necessary. *But never carry over a note to a second card.*

> **Write in your own words.** Summarize key points about a paragraph or section or restate the material in your own words. Avoid copying things word for word, but if you do...

> **...Put quotation marks around any material copied verbatim.** It's okay to include in your paper a sentence or paragraph written by someone else to emphasize a particular point (providing you do so on a limited basis). But you must copy such statements *exactly as written* in the original source—every word, every comma, every period. You must also enclose such material in quotation marks in your paper and credit the author.

ADD DETAIL TO YOUR NOTE CARDS

As you finish each note card, do the following:

> **In the upper left-hand corner of the card,** write down the resource number of the corresponding bibliography card (from its left-hand corner). This will remind you where you got the information.

> **Below the resource number,** write the page number(s) on which the information appeared.

> **Get out your preliminary outline.** Under which outline topic heading does the information on your card seem to fit? Jot the appropriate topic letter or Roman numeral in the upper right-hand corner of your note card.

> If you are unsure where the information fits into your outline, put an asterisk (*) instead of a topic letter or numeral. Later, when you do a more detailed outline, you can try to fit these "miscellaneous" note cards into specific areas.

> **Next to (or below) the topic letter,** jot down a one- or two-word "headline" that describes the information on the card.

> **When you have finished taking notes from a particular resource,** put a check mark on the bibliography card. This will let you know that you're done with that resource, at least for now.

Be sure that you transfer information accurately to your note cards. Double-check names, dates, and other statistics. As with your bibliography cards, it's not important that you put each of these elements in the exact places I've outlined here. You just need to be consistent. Always put the page number (resource number, topic heading, headline) in the same place, in the same manner.

ADD YOUR PERSONAL NOTES

Throughout your note-taking process, you may want to make some "personal" note cards, jotting down any thoughts, ideas, or impressions you have about your subject or your thesis.

Write each thought on a separate note card, just as you did with information taken from other resources. Assign your note card a topic heading and mini-headline, too. In the space where you would normally put the number of the resource, put your own initials or some other symbol to remind yourself that *you* were the source of the information or thought.

Congratulations. Presuming you have discovered a wide variety of pertinent resources and extracted a few dozen (or hundred) note cards of information from them, you are ready to take the next steps.

Chapter 8

Write great **papers**

"Writing has laws of perspective, of light and shade, just as painting does, or music. If you are born knowing them, fine. If not, learn them. Then rearrange the rules to suit yourself."

—TRUMAN CAPOTE

Your research is done.

That means at least *one-half* of your *paper*—perhaps as much as *three-quarters* of it—is done, even though you haven't (officially) written one word of the first draft.

It's time to organize your data. You need to decide if your temporary thesis is still on target, determine how you will organize your paper, and create a detailed outline.

Step 6: Prepare a detailed outline

This is where the note-card system really pays off. Your note cards give you a great tool for organizing your paper. Get out all of your note cards, then:

> ❭ Group together all of the cards that share the same outline topic letter or number (in the right-hand corner of each card).
> ❭ Put those different groups in order, according to your temporary outline.
> ❭ Within each topic group, sort the cards further. Group the cards that share the same "headline" (the two-word title in the upper-right corner).
> ❭ Go through your miscellaneous and personal cards, the ones you marked with an asterisk or symbol. Can you fit any of them into your existing topic groups? If so, replace the asterisk with the topic letter. If not, put the card at the very back of your stack.

Your note cards now should be organized according to your preliminary outline. Take a few minutes to read through your note cards, beginning at the front of the stack and moving through to the back. *What you are reading is a rough sketch of your paper*—the information you've collected in the order you (temporarily) plan to present it in your paper.

Does that order make sense? Would another arrangement work better? Here are some of the different organizational approaches you might consider for your paper:

> ❭ **Chronological.** Discusses events in the order in which they happened (by time of occurrence).
> ❭ **Spatial.** Presents information in geographical or physical order (from north to south, top to bottom, right to left, and so forth).
> ❭ **Numerical/Alphabetical.** An obvious way to organize a paper on "The Five Major Causes of Obesity" or "My Three Heroes."

> **Major division.** For topics that logically divide into obvious parts.
> **How to…**write a better paper, make a bookcase, repair a roof, do better on tests, and the like.
> **Problem/solution (*aka* cause/effect).** Presents a series of problems and possible solutions, discusses why something happened, or predicts what might happen as the result of a particular cause.
> **Effect/cause.** Discusses a condition, problem, or effect and works backward to what might have caused it.
> **Compare/contrast.** Discusses similarities and differences between people, things, or events. It may also be used when you want to discuss the advantages and disadvantages of a method, experiment, treatment, approach, and so on.
> **Order of importance.** Discusses the most important aspects of an issue first and continues through to the least important, or vice versa. (A slight variation of this is organizing your paper from the *known* to the *unknown*.)
> **Pro/con.** Arguments for and against a position, question, decision, approach, method, and so on.

The first four sequences are considered "natural," in that the organization is virtually demanded by the subject. The other sequences are "logical," in that the order is chosen and imposed by *you*, the writer.

Note that in many cases the actual order you choose is also reversible—you can move forward or backward in time, consider cause and effect or effect and cause, and so on. So you actually have a dozen and a half potential ways to organize your material!

Your subject and thesis may determine which organizational approach will work best. If you have a choice of more than one, use the one with which you're most comfortable or that you feel will be easiest for you to write. (Nobody says you *have* to choose the hardest way!) Keep in mind that you can use a *blend* of two approaches. For example, you might mention events in chronological order, then discuss the cause/effect of each.

If necessary, revise your general outline according to the organizational decision you have made. But *don't* change the letters or numerals you have assigned to the topics.

If you revised the order of your outline, just reorder your note cards so they fall in the same order as your new outline. Then go through each group of cards that share the same topic letter or number. Rearrange them so that they, too, follow the organizational pattern you chose.

After you sort all the cards that have been assigned a specific topic heading (A, B, C or I, II, III), review the cards you marked with an asterisk or personal symbol. Once again, try to figure out where they fit in your outline.

Don't force a card where it just doesn't belong. If the information it contains doesn't seem to fit anywhere, it's possible the data just isn't relevant to your revised thesis. Set it aside for now. You can try to include it again later.

And while you're setting aside inappropriate notes, don't forget to seek out "holes" in your paper—those areas that cry out for a more up-to-date fact, a good example, a stronger transition. No one likes to discover the need to do a little more research, but if *you've* noticed a problem, I guarantee your teacher will, too. Don't let a "black hole" turn a potentially great paper into one that's merely okay just because you don't want to spend another hour on research.

Now flip through your note cards from front to back. See that? You've created a detailed outline without even knowing it. The topic letters or numbers on your note cards match the main topics of your outline. And those headlines on your note cards? They're the subtopics for your outline. We simply transferred our note-card headlines to paper. They appear on our outline in the same order as our stack of cards.

Step 7: Write the first draft

How do you go about actually writing your term paper? As Lewis Carroll advised in *Alice's Adventures in Wonderland*: "'Begin at the beginning,' the King said, gravely, 'and go till you come to the end; then stop.'"

You may not have realized it, but you've already *done* a lot of the hard work that goes into the writing stage. You have thought about how your paper will flow, you have organized your notes, and you have prepared a detailed outline. All that's left is to transfer your information and ideas from note cards to paper.

Good writing takes concentration and thought. And concentration and thought require quiet—and lots of it! You need to have plenty of desk space, so you can spread out your note cards in front of you. Your work area should be well-lit. And you should have a dictionary and thesaurus close at hand. If possible, write directly on to your computer, so you can add, delete, and rearrange your words with a click.

Remember: At this point, your goal is to produce a rough draft—with emphasis on the word "rough." Your first draft isn't supposed to be perfect. It's *supposed* to need revision.

If you go into this thinking you're going to turn out a teacher-ready paper on your first try, you're doomed. That kind of performance pressure leads only to anxiety and frustration.

As important as they are, the essence of good writing has little to do with grammar, spelling, punctuation, and the like. The essence of good writing is good thinking.

Your thoughts, ideas, and logic are the foundation of your paper. And you need to build a house's foundation before you worry about hanging the front door. So, for now, just concentrate on getting your thoughts on paper. Don't worry about using exactly the "right" word. Don't worry about getting commas in all the right places. We'll take care of all that polishing later.

Your note cards helped you come up with a detailed outline. Now, they're going to help you plot out the actual paragraphs and sentences of your paper:

> Arrange your notecards in the same order as your detailed outline. Take out those labeled with the letter or number of the first topic on your outline.

> Out of that stack, take out all the cards marked with the same "headline" as the first subheading in your outline.

> Look at the information on those cards. Think about how the various pieces of information might fit together in a paragraph.

> Rearrange those cards so they fall in the order you have determined is best for the paragraph.

> Continue to do this for each group of cards until you reach the end of the deck.

Each paragraph in your paper is like a mini-essay. It should have a topic sentence—a statement of the key point or fact you will discuss in the paragraph—and contain the evidence to support it. This evidence can come in different forms, such as quotes from experts, research statistics, examples from your research or your own experience, detailed descriptions, or other background information.

Stack up your paragraphs like bricks into your own "wall of evidence." Construct each paragraph carefully, and your readers will have no choice but to agree with your final conclusion.

If paragraphs are the bricks, transitions—which move the reader from one thought to another—are the mortar holding them together. Smooth transitions help readers move effortlessly from one thought to another.

Double- or triple-space your draft—that will make it easier to edit later. After you are finished with a note card, put a check mark at the bottom and put it aside.

If you decide that you won't include information from a particular card, don't throw it away...yet. Keep it in a separate stack. You may decide to fit in that piece of information in another part of your paper or change your mind after you read your rough draft and decide to include the information where you had originally planned.

And if you get stuck

Got writer's block already? Here are a few tricks to get you unstuck.

> Pretend you're writing a letter to a good friend. Just tell him or her everything you've learned about your subject and why you believe your thesis is correct.

> Use everyday language. Too many people get so hung up on using fancy words and phrases that

they forget that their goal is communication. Simpler is better.

> Type *some*thing...*any*thing. Once you have written that first sentence—even if it's an *atrocious* paragraph—your brain will start to generate spontaneous ideas.

> Don't edit yourself! As you write your rough draft, don't keep beating yourself up with negative thoughts. Remember, your goal is just a *rough* draft; I guarantee parts of it will need serious rewriting!

> Keep moving. If you get hung up in a particular section, don't sit there stewing over it for hours ...or even many minutes. Just write a quick note about what you plan to cover in that section, then go on to the next section. Try to make it all the way through your paper with as few stops as possible.

Try freewriting and brainstorming

Focused freewriting and brainstorming are two methods used by professional writers when the waters of creativity are dammed up somewhere in their brains. While similar, there are a couple of important differences between the two methods of getting started.

In both cases, set a brief time limit (perhaps 10 or 15 minutes), summarize your main topic in a phrase or sentence to get your thoughts moving, and do not edit or even review what you have written until the time is up.

Brainstorming is writing down everything you can think of *that relates to the topic*. It does not require that you work in any sequence or that your notes be logical or even reasonable.

Asking yourself questions about the topic, no matter how strange, may help you generate new ideas.

In focused freewriting, the emphasis is on writing... *anything*...without worrying about whether what you put down is even vaguely related to your topic. The key is just to start writing—a diary entry, the biography of your dog, your thoughts about current rock videos—and *not to stop* until the time is up.

Brainstorming is useful when you are ready to write but just can't get a handle on exactly where to begin. Freewriting is useful when you can't get your brain to work at all. Both methods will help you start writing, which is all you are trying to do.

Document your sources

To avoid plagiarism, you must document the source when you put any of the following in your paper:

> Quotations taken from a published source.
> Someone else's theories or ideas.
> Someone else's sentences, phrases, or special expressions.
> Facts, figures, and research data compiled by someone else.
> Graphs, pictures, and charts designed by someone else.

There are some exceptions. You don't need to document the source of a fact, theory, or expression that is common knowledge. And you do not need a source note when you use a phrase or expression for which there is no known author.

To judge whether a statement needs a source note, ask yourself whether readers would otherwise think that you had come up with the information or idea all by yourself. If the answer is yes, you need a source note. If you're in doubt, include a source note anyway.

For many years, the preferred way to credit sources was the footnote. Two other forms of documentation, endnotes and parenthetical notes, are popular now as well.

A footnote is a source note that appears at the bottom of a page of text. You put a raised (superscript) number at the end of the statement or fact you need to document, which tells your readers to look at the bottom of the page for a note about the source of the data.

What goes in a footnote? The same information that's in the bibliography listing *and* the exact page number the information appears on.

In front of that source note, put the same superscript number you put next to the statement or fact in your text.

There is no limit to the number of footnotes you may have in your paper. Number each footnote consecutively, starting with the number 1. For every footnote "flag" in your paper, be sure there is a corresponding source note at the bottom of the page, parenthetically within the text, or end of the paper.

Like bibliography listings, different authorities cite different rules for setting up footnotes. Ask your teacher whose rules you are to follow.

Step 8: Do additional research

Did you discover any gaps in your research as you cobbled together your first draft? Identify questions that you need additional information to answer? Then now is the time to find whatever additional information you need.

Step 9: Write the second draft

The goal for this phase is to edit for meaning—improve the flow of your paper, organize your thoughts better, clarify confusing points, and strengthen weak arguments.

As you review your rough draft, ask yourself the following questions:

> Do your thoughts move logically from one point to the next?

> Is the meaning of every sentence and paragraph crystal clear?

> Does every sentence make a point—or support one?

> Do you move smoothly from one paragraph to the next?

> Do you support your conclusions with solid evidence—research data, examples, statistics?

> Do you include a good *mix* of evidence—quotes from experts, scientific data, personal experiences, historical examples?

> Do you have a solid introduction and conclusion?

> Did you write in your own words and style, not merely string together phrases and quotes "borrowed" from other authors?

> Have you explained your subject thoroughly, or assumed that readers have more knowledge about it than they actually might? (Remember: *You're* familiar with the topic now, but just because something is now obvious to you doesn't mean your readers will know what you're talking about.)

> ❯ Have you convinced your readers that your thesis is valid?
> ❯ Is there information that, while correct and informative, just doesn't belong? Cut it out!
> ❯ Have you maintained a consistent point of view (that is, first, second, or third person throughout)?
> ❯ Does your last paragraph successfully summarize the entire paper and effectively "close" your argument?

Mark any trouble spots with a colored pencil or pen or track them on your computer. If you have an idea on how to fix a section, jot it down on your rough draft. Now sit down and begin to rewrite. Focus on all of those problem areas you found. If necessary, add new information. Play with sentences, paragraphs, even entire sections.

Rework your opening and closing paragraphs

"I always do the first line well, but I have trouble doing the others."

—MOLIERE

When you feel you have created a wonderful paper, examine your opening and closing paragraphs. Take the time to go over these—again and again—and keep polishing them. More than one "OK-not-great" paper has earned a better-than-expected grade because of an "A+" introduction and conclusion.

Your paper's opening paragraph is the most important of all. It sets out what you will be arguing for or against (and why you chose that side) and introduces the rest of the paper. If it's well written, it will seamlessly lead your teacher into the rest of the paper *and* earn you points for solid organization. If it's poorly written, it may not matter what follows—your teacher may conclude you obviously don't know what you're talking about and grade accordingly (while spending less time than he might have otherwise on the rest of the paper).

Think of the introduction and the conclusion as the bread of a sandwich; the information in between is the hamburger, lettuce, tomato, and pickle. What's in the middle may be the main attraction, but without the bread you can't even call it a sandwich.

Here are some ways to start off your paper with a little zing:

> Say something that grabs attention.
> Say something controversial.
> Paint a picture of a scene.
> Recreate an event.
> Use a potent quote.
> Ask a provocative question.

But don't—absolutely do *not*—open with a joke. The joke will be on you. Most teachers have no sense of humor once they start grading papers (presuming they did before).

Check all your facts

When you finish editing for content and meaning, print or type a clean copy of your paper, then double-check all of your facts for accuracy:

> Did you spell names, terms, and places correctly?
> When you quoted dates and statistics, did you get your numbers straight?
> Do you have a source note (or preliminary source note) for every fact, expression, or idea that is not your own?

> If you quoted material from a source, did you quote that source exactly, word for word, comma for comma, and did you put the material in quotation marks?

Mark any corrections on your new draft.

Keep rewriting

Now take an even closer look at all your sentences and paragraphs. Try to make them smoother, tighter, and easier to understand:

> Use action verbs and the active voice: "Apes in captivity can survive for 30 years or more" is better than "Ages of 30 years or more may be reached by apes in captivity."

> Is there too much fat? Seize every opportunity to make the same point in fewer words.

> Are there places where phrasing or construction is awkward? Try to rearrange the sentence or section so that it flows more smoothly.

> Did you use descriptive, colorful words? Did you tell your reader "The planes were damaged" or paint a more descriptive picture: "The planes were broken-down hulks of rusted metal— bullet-ridden, neglected warbirds that could barely limp down the runway"?

> Consult a thesaurus for synonyms that work better than the words you originally chose. But don't get carried away and use words so obscure that the average reader wouldn't know their meaning. When in doubt, opt for the familiar word rather than the obscure, the shorter vs. the longer, the tangible vs. the hypothetical, the direct word vs. the roundabout phrase.

> Have you overused cliches or slang expressions?
> Especially in academic writing, they are not par-
> ticularly appreciated. Your paper may be "dead
> as a doornail" if you don't "get the lead out," get
> rid of some of the "oldies but goodies," and make
> sure your paper is "neat as a pin."

> Have you overused particular words? Constantly
> using the same words makes your writing bor-
> ing. Check a thesaurus for other possibilities.

> How do the words *sound?* When you read your
> paper aloud, does it flow like a rhythmic piece
> of music or plod along like a funeral dirge?

> Vary the length of your sentences and para-
> graphs to make your writing more exciting. Mix
> short, simple sentences with complex sen-
> tences (an independent clause and one or more
> dependent clauses), and embedded sentences
> (combining two clauses using relative pronouns
> rather than conjunctions).

> Always remember the point of the paper—to
> communicate your ideas as clearly and concisely
> as possible. So don't get lost in the details. If you
> have to choose between that "perfect" word and
> the most organized paper imaginable, opt for the
> latter.

Step 10: Prepare your final bibliography

Your bibliography should be at the end of your paper, on a
separate page or pages:

> One inch from the top of the page, center the
> title "Works Cited" or "Works Consulted,"
> depending upon which type of bibliography
> you're preparing.

> Use the same margins as you did for the rest of your paper—one inch all the way around.

> Treat your bibliography pages as if they are a continuation of the text of your paper and number them accordingly—*don't* start repaginating.

> List sources alphabetically, by the author's last name. If no author is given, list by the first word in the title of the work (unless the first word is "A," "An," or "The," in which case list by the second word of the title).

> The first line of each listing should be flush with the left margin. Indent all other lines five spaces from the left margin.

> Double-space all listings and double-space between entries.

> Abbreviate all months except May, June, and July.

Step 11: Check spelling and grammar

I've told you your thoughts are the most important element of your paper. And they are. But it's also true that glaring mistakes in grammar and spelling will lead your teacher to believe that you are either careless or downright ignorant—neither of which will bode well for your final grade.

So get out your dictionary and a reference book on English usage and grammar. Scour your paper, sentence by sentence, marking corrections with your colored pen or pencil. Look for:

> *Misspelled words.* Check every word. Sound-alike words may elude your computer's spell-check program. "There" might be spelled correctly, but not if you meant to write "their."

> *Incorrect punctuation.* Review the rules for placement of commas, quotation marks, periods, and other punctuation. Make sure you follow those rules throughout your paper.
> *Incorrect sentence structure.* Look for dangling participles, split infinitives, sentences that end in prepositions, and other grammatical no-no's.

Here are a couple of tricks of the trade: Read your paper aloud. Go ahead—shout it from the rooftops! It's amazing how easily you'll discover misplaced words, poor grammar, even a misspelling or two. Or read your paper backward. This forces you to focus on each individual word and is a sensational way to pick up misspellings.

Step 12: Have someone *else* proofread

Reprint your paper, making all those corrections you marked during the last step. Format the paper according to the teacher's instructions. Incorporate your final footnotes and bibliography.

Give your paper a title, one that's short and to the point but tells readers what they can expect to learn from your paper.

Proof it *again*, then find someone else who is a good proofreader—a parent, relative, or friend—and ask him or her to proofread it.

Steps 13, 14, and 15: The final draft

Incorporate any changes or errors you or your proofreader caught. Type or print a final draft. *Proof it again*—very carefully.

Put your paper in a new manuscript binder or folder. Then, turn it in—on time, of course!

Oral reports

There are some key differences between writing a report and presenting it orally, especially if you don't want to make the mistake of just reading your report in front of the class.

If you've been assigned to give a talk for a class, it will probably fall into one of the following categories:

> *Exposition:* a straightforward statement of facts.
> *Argument:* trying to change the opinions of at least a portion of the audience.
> *Description:* providing a visual picture to your listeners.
> *Narration:* storytelling.

The most common forms of oral reports assigned in school will be exposition and argument. You'll find that you will research and organize information for these types of speeches pretty much the way you would a term paper.

As you gather information for your report, making notes on index cards as you did for your term paper, keep this in mind: In order for you to be effective, you must use some different techniques when you *tell* your story rather than *write* it. Here are a few:

> *Don't make your topic too broad.* This advice, offered for preparing written reports as well, is even more important when preparing a talk. Try giving an effective speech on "Thomas Edison," "Jane Austen's novels," or "the Civil War" in 15 minutes, the usual amount of time assigned for oral reports. These topics are more suited to a series of books!

"Thomas Edison's three greatest inventions," "The way the movie *Clueless* failed to meet the standards set by Austen's *Emma*," or "The effect of the Gettysburg Address on Southern morale" are more manageable topics. Narrowing the scope of your talk will help you research and organize it more effectively.

> *Don't overuse statistics.* While they're very important for lending credibility, too many will weigh down your speech and bore your audience.

> *Anecdotes add color and life to your talk.* But use them sparingly, because they can slow down your speech. Get to the punch line before the yawns start.

> *Be careful with quotes.* Unlike a term paper, a speech allows you to establish yourself as an authority with less fear of being accused of plagiarism. So you can present a lot more facts without attribution. (But you'd better have the sources in case you're asked about your facts.)

I've found that trying to shuffle a bunch of papers in front of a class is difficult and that note cards that fit in the palm of my hand are a lot easier to use, but only if the notes on them are very short and to the point. Then they act as "triggers" rather than verbatim cue cards. The shorter the notes—and the more often you practice your report so each note triggers the right information—the more effective your report will be. (And the less you will have to look at them, making eye contact with your class and teacher easier.)

Here are four other ways to make oral reports more effective:

> ❯ Take a deep breath before you go to the front of the class. And don't worry about pausing, even taking another deep breath or two, if you lose your place or find your confidence slipping.

> ❯ Pick out one person to talk to—preferably a friend, but an animated and/or interested person will do—and direct your talk at him or her.

> ❯ Practice, practice, *practice* your presentation. Jangled nerves are often the result of a lack of confidence. The better you know your material, the less nervous you'll be and the better and more spontaneous your presentation.

> ❯ If you suffer from involuntary "shakes" at the mere thought of standing in front of a roomful of people, make sure there is a lectern, desk, or something else you can cling to.

If every trick in the world still doesn't steady your nerves, consider taking a public speaking course (Dale Carnegie, *et al*), joining the Toastmasters Club, or seeking out similar extracurricular help.

'Twas the night before the deadline...

Despite my best advice, some of you will undoubtedly choose to delay working on your paper until the last possible instant. Many of you may well suffer from the same feelings of malaise and procrastination that infected much of my dorm when papers were due. A lot of my friends seemed hell-bent on finding something, *any*thing, that could be done instead of actually sitting down and writing that flaming paper.

I received this exaggerated but all-too-familiar "paper writing plan" via e-mail from a colleague's fraternity. Does it sound like your systematic approach? Do you believe it's a valid way to proceed? Have I been writing all this for nothing?

How to Write a Paper

1. Sit in a straight, comfortable chair in a well-lighted place with plenty of freshly sharpened pencils.
2. Carefully read over the assignment. Underline or highlight key instructions.
3. Walk down to the vending machines and buy some coffee so you can concentrate.
4. On the way back to your room, stop and visit with your friend from class. If he hasn't started *his* paper either, walk to the nearest convenience store and buy a sugary treat to give you some energy. If, instead, he proudly shows off his paper-typed, double-spaced, and bound in one of those irritating see-thru plastic folders—hurt him.
5. When you get back to your room, sit in a straight, comfortable chair in a clean well-lighted place with plenty of freshly sharpened pencils.
6. Read over the assignment again to make absolutely certain you understand it. Highlight it in a different color.
7. You know, you haven't written to that kid you met at camp since fourth grade—better write that letter now and get it out of the way so you can concentrate.
8. Inspect your teeth in the bathroom mirror. Floss. Twice.

9. Listen to your favorite CD. And that's it. I mean it. As soon as it's over, start writing that paper.

10. Listen to another CD.

11. Rearrange all your CDs into alphabetical order.

12. Phone your friend to see if *he's* started writing yet. Exchange derogatory remarks about your teacher, the course, the university, and the world at large.

13. Sit in a straight, comfortable chair in a clean well-lighted place with plenty of freshly sharpened pencils.

14. Read over the assignment again; roll the words across your tongue; savor their special flavor. Choose at least three more highlighter colors.

15. Check the newspaper listings to make sure you aren't missing something truly worthwhile on TV. **NOTE:** When you have a paper due in less than 12 hours, anything on TV—from a serious documentary to any iteration of *Desperate Housewives* or *Law & Order*—is truly worthwhile.

16. Look at your tongue in the bathroom mirror.

17. Sit down and do some serious thinking about your plans for the future.

18. Open your door; check to see if there are any mysterious, trench-coated strangers lurking in the hall.

19. Sit in a straight, comfortable chair in a clean, well-lighted place with plenty of freshly sharpened pencils.

20. Read over the assignment one more time, just for the heck of it.

21. Scoot your chair across the room to the window and watch the sunrise.
22. Lie face down on the floor. Moan and thrash about.
23. Leap up and write that paper as fast as you can type!

If this approach is even remotely close to what *you* actually do, please reread chapters 7 and 8 again...but do not choose a different colored highlighter.

Chapter 9

Ace any Test

Throughout your educational life—and, more than likely, the *rest* of your life—testing will be an inevitable if sometimes frightening and distressing reality. The sooner you learn the techniques of preparing for, taking, and mastering tests, the better off you'll be.

What do they want to know?

Many tests are as much a measure of the *way* you study—your ability to organize a mountain of material—as they are a measure of your knowledge of the material itself. This is especially true of any test that purports to measure knowledge spread across the years and your mastery of such a broad spectrum of material—the SAT; GRE; bar or medical exam; exams for nurses, CPAs, financial planners; and others. Which means the better you *study*, the better your *score* will probably be on such tests.

Before you can decide *how* to study for a particular test, it's imperative that you know exactly what you're being tested *on.* Preparing a midterm or final exam requires a different approach than studying for a weekly quiz. And the biggest final of your life is child's play compared to "monster tests" like the oral exams I faced before they allowed me to graduate college—which covered everything I was supposed to have learned in four years.

Studying for a standardized test like the SAT, ACT, or GRE is also completely different—you can't pull out your textbook and, knowing what chapters are being included, just "bone up."

The structure of the test is also of paramount importance, not necessarily in terms of how you study, but how you tackle it right from the start.

What are you afraid of?

Tests can be scary creatures. So before I start doling out test-taking techniques, let's tackle one of the key problems many of you will face—test anxiety, a reaction characterized by sweaty palms, a blank mind, and the urge to flee to Fiji on the next available cargo ship.

What does it mean when someone proclaims she doesn't "test well"? It may mean she doesn't *study* well (or, at the very least, *prepare* well). It could mean she is easily distracted, unprepared for the type of test she is confronting, or simply unprepared mentally to take *any* test.

We all recognize the competitive nature of tests. Some of us rise to the occasion when facing such a challenge. Others succumb to the pressure. Both reactions probably have little to do with one's level of knowledge, relative intelligence, or amount of preparation. The smartest students in your class may be the ones most afraid of tests.

You are certainly not alone

Very few people look forward to a test; more of you are afraid of tests than you'd think. But that doesn't mean you *have* to fear them.

Few people enter a testing site cool, calm, and ready for action. Most of us have various butterflies gamboling in our stomachs, sweat glands operating in overdrive, and a sincere desire to be somewhere else...*anywhere* else.

The more pressure you put on yourself—the larger you allow a test (and, of course, your hoped-for good score) to loom in your own mind—the less you are helping yourself. (And the bigger the test really *is*, the more likely you are to keep reminding yourself of its importance.)

Let's face it: Your scores on some tests *can* have a major effect on where you go to college, whether you go to graduate school, whether you get the job you want. But no matter how important a test may be to your career, it is just as important to *de-emphasize* that test's importance in your mind. This should have no effect on your preparation—you should still study as if your life depended on a superior score. It might!

Keeping the whole experience in perspective might also help: Twenty years from now, nobody will remember, or care, what you scored on *any* test—no matter how life-determining you feel that test is right now.

Of course, you *can* make it easier to do all this by *not* going out of your way—certainly before an especially big or important test—to pile *more* stress atop an already stressful event. Two days before the SAT is *not* the time to dump a boyfriend, move, change jobs, take out a big loan, or create any other waves in your normally placid river of life.

Some people thrive on their own misery and are jealous if you don't feed on it, too. They want to suck you into their gloom, whether you really know or care what's happening.

So watch out for those "friends" who call you the night before the exam and shriek, "I just found out we have to know Chapter 12!" Don't fall into their trap. Instead of dialing 911, calmly remind them that the printed sheet the professor passed out two weeks ago clearly says that the test will cover chapters 6 through 11. Then hang up, get on with your life, and let them wring their hands all the way to the bottom of the grading sheet. (Of course, if *you* don't bother to check what's going to be on the test, a call like this *will* panic you ...and waste your time.)

How to reduce your anxiety

To come to terms with the "importance" of a test, read the following list. Knowing the answers to as many of these questions as possible will help reduce your anxiety.

> What material will the exam cover?
> How many total points are possible?
> What percentage of my semester grade is based on this exam?
> How much time will I have to take the exam?
> Where will the exam be held?
> What kinds of questions will be on the exam (matching, multiple-choice, essay, true/false, and so forth)?
> How many of each type of question will be on the exam?
> How many points will be assigned to each question?
> Will certain types of questions count more than others?

> ❯ Will it be an open-book exam?
> ❯ What can I take in with me? Calculator? Candy bar? Other material crucial to my success?
> ❯ Will I be penalized for wrong answers?

You've already found that scheduling breaks during your study routine makes it easier for you to focus on your books and complete your assignments faster and with more concentration. Scheduling breaks during the test itself has the same effect.

No matter what the time limits or pressures, don't feel you cannot afford such a brief respite. You may need it *most* when you're convinced you can *least* afford it, just as those who most need time management techniques "just don't have the time" to learn them.

If your mind is a jumble of facts and figures, names and dates, you may find it difficult to zero in on the specific details you need to recall, even if you know all the material backward and forward. The adrenaline rushing through your system may just make "instant retrieval" impossible.

The simplest relaxation technique is deep breathing. Lean back in your chair, relax your muscles, and take three very deep breaths (count to 10 while you hold each one).

There are a variety of meditation techniques that may also work for you. Each is based on a similar principle: focusing your mind on one thing to the exclusion of everything else. While you're concentrating on the object of your meditation (even if the object is a nonsense word or a spot on the wall), your mind can't think about anything else, which allows it to slow down a bit.

The next time you can't focus during a test, try sitting back, taking three deep breaths, and concentrating for a minute or two on the word "RON." When you're done, you should be in a far more relaxed state and ready to tackle the next section.

Prepare for great test scores

Some rites of preparation are pertinent to any test, from a weekly quiz to the SAT and everything in between.

Plan ahead

I admit it. When I was a student, even in college, my attention span tended to be bounded by weekends. Tell me in October that there'd be a big test the first week of December and I'd remember, oh, around November 30th.

Of such habits are cramming, crib sheets, and failing marks made.

The key to avoiding all of these unpleasantries is *regular, periodic review*. Spending 30 minutes a day for six days studying for an upcoming test is preferable to cramming all your studying into a three-hour block the night before. The more often you review, the less often you will have to pull all-nighters the week of the test. You already will have stayed on top of the material, written down and asked questions that arose from your reviews, and gone over class and textbook notes to make sure you understand everything. Your last-minute review will be relatively leisurely and organized, not feverish and chaotic.

Sorry we missed you

Doing poorly on a test is discouraging. Doing poorly on a test you felt ready for is depressing. Missing the test entirely is devastating. It's imperative that you know when and where all tests are scheduled and allow ample time to get to them.

If you're still in high school, getting to a particular test shouldn't be too hard—it will probably be held during your regular class period in your normal classroom. But in college, tests may be scheduled at hours different than the normal class period...and at entirely different sites.

Likewise, major out-of-school tests like the SAT and ACT may not even be held at your school. In such cases, make sure you allow enough time to drive to, or be driven to, wherever you have to be—especially if you're not quite sure how to get there!

As soon as you know the time and location of any major test, enter it on your calendar. Whether in high school, college, or grad school, most schools set aside a week, two, or even more for final exams. This exam period is usually clearly marked in your college handbook, announced in class (usually on the first day), and included in your class syllabus.

Make optional assignments mandatory

Sometimes, in addition to your regular reading and other assignments, the teacher will assign optional reading at the beginning of a course. These books, articles, and monographs may never be discussed in any class—but material from them may be included on a test, especially a final exam. If you have neglected to add this supplementary reading to your schedule, but wish to read some or all of these items before the test, make sure you allow enough time to find them. A lot of other students may have also left such reading to the last minute, and you may be unable to find the material you need if you wait too long.

Pack accordingly

Lastly, bring whatever materials you need to the test, from pens and pencils to calculators. I also recommend—especially for a long test like the SAT, ACT, or many final exams—that you bring along a candy bar, hard candies, a granola bar, or some other "quick energy" snack to help wake you up when you need to give yourself a figurative slap in the face.

Although many testing booklets will include room for notes, it may not be sufficient for your purposes. If you are expected to answer three, five, or even more essay questions, you will want a lot of scratch paper to outline and organize your thoughts. Likewise, a particularly complex math test may quickly use up every square inch of margin. So bring along a separate writing tablet or even a stack of scrap paper. There are few situations in which their use won't be allowed.

If you didn't listen before...

Review, review, review. If you don't follow my advice for periodic review, set aside the time to review and study a week or two before the test, especially for midterms and finals. Most colleges—and many high schools—offer a reading or study period, usually the week before midterms or finals, when no classes are scheduled and library hours are often extended. Take advantage of this time.

Some helpful teachers may offer formal review sessions before big exams. Attending these and listening carefully to a teacher's points of emphasis may help you further identify material that is sure to be on the test.

The more material you need to review, the more important it is to clear your schedule. A four-, five-, or six-course load covering dozens of books, plus lectures and discussions, papers and projects, will easily generate hundreds of pages of notes. Reviewing, understanding, and studying them will require your full-time effort for a week, even two. So make sure all other end-of-term work, especially major projects and papers, are out of the way.

Whether you need to schedule a solid two weeks for a complete review or just two or three days because you have already reviewed most of your course work on a regular basis, allow more time for the subjects in which you are weakest.

Organize your material

> Gather all the material you have been using for the course: books, workbooks, handouts, notes, homework, and previous tests and papers.

> Compare the contents with the material you will be tested on and ask yourself: What exactly do I need to review for this test?

> Select the material for review. Reducing the pile of books and papers will be a psychological aid—it'll seem as if you have more than enough time and energy to study for the test.

> Hot tip: Make a crib sheet as if you were going to cheat on the test, which, of course, you aren't. Use it for last-minute review. If you are lucky enough to get an open-book test, thank me!

Schedule the time you need

Consider the following when deciding how much time to study for a particular test:

> *How much time do I usually spend studying for this type of exam?* What have been the results? If you usually spend three hours and you consistently get Ds, perhaps you need to reassess the time you're spending or, more accurately, *mis*spending.

> *What grade do I have going for me now?* If it's a solid B and you're convinced you can't get an A, you may decide to devote *less* time to this test and more to a subject in which you have a better

> *shot at a top grade. If you have a C+ and a good
> grade on the exam would give you a solid B, you
> may decide to devote more time to *this* subject.*

> ❯ *What special studying do I have to do?* It's one
> thing to review notes and practice with a study
> group, but if you need to sit in a language lab
> and listen to hours of tapes or run the slower
> group of gerbils through the maze yet again,
> plan accordingly.

> ❯ *Organize the materials* you need to study, pace
> yourself, and check to see how much material
> you have covered in the first hour of review.
> How does this compare to what you have left to
> study? Not every hour will be equally produc-
> tive, but you should be able to project the time
> you need based on what you are able to accom-
> plish in an hour.

Cramming doesn't work

We have all done it at one time or another, with one excuse or
another—waited until the last minute and then tried to cram
a week's or month's or entire semester's worth of work into a
single night or weekend. Did it work for you? I didn't think so.

The reality is that cramming works—on one level—for
a small minority of students. Somehow, they're able to shove
more "stuff" into short-term memory than the rest of us and
actually remember it, at least for 24 hours. After those 24
hours? Gone with the wind. Which means if they managed
to do well on a weekly quiz, all that cramming didn't do them
a bit of good for the upcoming midterm or final.

The rest of us don't even get that smidgen of good news—
after a night of no sleep and too much coffee, we're lucky if

we remember where the test *is* the next morning. Some hours later, trying to stay awake long enough to make it back to bed, we not only haven't learned anything, we haven't even done very well on the test we crammed for!

That's probably the best reason of all not to cram—it probably won't work!

How to cram anyway

Nevertheless, despite your resolve, best intentions, and firm conviction that cramming is a losing proposition, you may well find yourself—though hopefully not too often—in the position of needing to do *some*thing the night before a test you haven't studied for at all. If so, there are some rules to follow that will make your night of cramming at least marginally successful:

Be realistic about what you can do. You absolutely *cannot* master an entire semester's worth of work in a single night, especially if your class attendance has been sporadic (or non-existent) and you've skimmed two books out of a syllabus of two dozen. The *more* information you try to cram in, the *less* effective you will be.

Being realistic means soberly assessing your situation—you're hanging by your thumbs and are just trying to avoid falling into that vat of boiling oil. Avoiding the oil, saving the damsel in distress, and inheriting the kingdom—acing the test—may be a bit too much to wish for, no matter whom your Fairy Godmother is.

Be selective and study in depth. The more classes you've managed to miss and assignments you've failed to complete, the more selective you need to be in organizing your cram session. So you must identify, as best you can, the topics you are sure will be on the test. Then study only *those*. It's better in this case to know a lot about a little rather than a little about a lot. You may get lucky and pick the three topics the three essays cover!

Massage your memory. Use every memory technique in Chapter 4 to maximize what you're able to retain in your short-term memory.

Know when to surrender. When you can't remember your name or stay focused, give up and get some sleep.

Consider an early morning rather than a late-night cram, especially if you're a "morning" person. I've found it more effective to go to bed and get up early rather than go to bed late and wake up exhausted.

When you arrive at the test site, spend the first few minutes writing down whatever you remember and are afraid you'll forget.

When in doubt, ask

Yes, there are teachers who test you on the most mundane details of their course, requiring you to review every book, every note, every scribble.

However, I don't think most teachers work that way. You will more than likely be tested on some subset of the course—those particular topics, problems, or facts and figures the teacher believes most important.

How do you know what those are? To put it bluntly, how do you know what's going to be on the test?

Teachers give many clues. In general, the more often you see or hear the same material, the more important it probably is and the more likely that it will show up on a test.

A fact or topic need not be repeated in order to scream "Learn me!" Just as you learned to watch a teacher's body language and listen for verbal clues to identify note-worthy topics, you'll learn to identify topics the teacher indicates—nonverbally—are the most important. Your teacher's attitude toward note-taking may tip you off, as well. If he or she requires you to take detailed notes—even wants them turned in (sometimes in high school, rarely in college)—I'd figure that she considers the material she covers in class more important than the textbook(s). Study accordingly.

Have you saved earlier tests and quizzes from that class? Returned exams, especially if they contain a lot of comments from your teacher, should give you an excellent indication of where to concentrate your study time.

Is it wrong to ask the teacher what kind of test to expect? Absolutely not. Will he or she always tell you? Absolutely not. If you have access to old exams written by the same teacher, especially if they cover the same material you're going to be tested on, use *them* for review.

Why? Like most of us, teachers are creatures of habit. Don't expect the same questions to appear again. No teacher is *that* accommodating. But the way the test is prepared, the kinds of questions employed, and the mix of questions (100 true/false, 50 multiple-choice, and one—count 'em—one essay) will give a much better idea of what to expect on your test.

And see if you can find others who had this teacher last year or last semester. Can they give you any advice, tips, hints, or warnings?

Some teachers love one type of question. Some are true/false freaks; others push the multiple-choice/short answer combo. If old tests, former students, the teacher's own comments about an upcoming test, and your own experience tell you this is true, you might as well study for that kind of test. You still have to know the material, of course. It's just that you may need to remind yourself that you're going to have to deal with it in a particular fashion.

Many teachers use a combination of test questions to find out what you know. Frankly, some of them hate grading essay questions, so they rarely use them. Others prefer essay questions because:

> They are quicker and easier to prepare.
> They may be preferred when a group is small and the test will not be reused.
> They are used to explore students' attitudes rather than measure their achievements.
> They are used to encourage and reward the development of the students' skill in writing.
> They are suitable when it's important for the students to explain or describe.
> They are more suitable to some material. You're likely to have more essay questions in English and history than you are in the sciences.

Some teachers prefer objective questions because:

> They are preferred when the group is large and the test may be reused.
> They are more efficient when highly reliable test scores must be obtained quickly.
> They are more suitable for covering a larger amount of content in the same amount of time.
> They are easier for the teacher to give an impartial grade. Every student has to write down "C" to get number 22 correct.
> They are easier for some teachers to create.
> They may be used when students need to demonstrate or show work.

Never study everything

Once you've discovered the type of test facing you, you need to figure out what's actually going to be *on* it (and, hence, what you actually need to study). Remember: it's rarely, if ever, "everything."

Conduct a cursory review of the material you are convinced is not important enough to be included on an upcoming test. This will automatically give you more time to concentrate on those areas you're sure *will* be included.

Then create a "To Study" sheet for each test. On it, list specific books to review, notes to recheck, and topics, principles, ideas, and concepts to go over. Then check off each item as you study it. This is akin to breaking the paper-writing process into smaller, easier-to-accomplish steps and will have the same effect—to minimize procrastination, logically organize your studying, and give you ongoing "jolts" of accomplishment as you complete each item.

Test yourself

Just as you have made it a habit to write down questions as you study your texts, why not try to construct your own tests? The harder you make them, the better prepared and more confident you will be when you confront the real test.

Practice tests offer some real advantages, whether you're studying for a weekly quiz, the SAT, or your bar exam. In fact, the longer and more "standardized" the test, the more important it is to be familiar with its structure, rules, and traps.

First and foremost, familiarizing yourself with the type of test you're taking will enable you to strategically study the material (prioritize) and strategically attack the test (organize).

Familiarization breeds comfort, and being comfortable—*relaxed*—is a key component to doing well.

Familiarization also breeds organization, allowing you to concentrate on the test itself and not on its structure. This gives you more time to actually *take* the test rather than figure it out. It also reduces the effect of whatever time constraints the test imposes on you.

Last but not least, taking practice tests is a highly effective way to study and remember the material.

Test-day rules and reminders

If the test is not scheduled during a regular class period, make sure to arrive at the test site early. Based on your preferences (from Chapter 2), sit where you like.

Be careful, however. There may be some variations you have to take into account. In a test where there are 200 or 300 people in a room, there is a distinct advantage to sitting up front: You can hear the instructions and the answers to questions better, and you generally get the test first (and turn it in last).

If you have permission to look through the entire test, do so. Give yourself an overview of what lies ahead. That way you can spot the easier sections and get an idea of the point values assigned to each section.

Know the ground rules

Will you be penalized for guessing? The teacher may inform you that you will earn two points for every correct answer but *lose* one point for every incorrect one. This will certainly affect whether you guess or skip the question—or, at the very least, how many potential answers you feel you need to eliminate before the odds of guessing are in your favor.

In the case of a standardized test like the SAT, ACT, or GRE, read the instructions on a previous test before you go to the test site. (There are numerous prep books that include "actual tests.") Then just skim the instructions in your booklet or on the computer to make sure nothing has changed. This may save you minutes—precious time during any such test.

Are the questions or sections weighted? Some tests may have many sections, some of which count for very little—10 or 15 percent of your final score. Another part, usually a major essay, may be more heavily weighted—30 percent or more of your grade. This should clearly influence the amount of time and energy you devote to each section.

Draw your way through

Throughout a test, don't miss an opportunity to draw a picture for yourself if it helps you understand the question or figure out the right answer. If the question deals with any sort of cause-and-effect relationship that contains several steps, draw or write down those steps very quickly, using abbreviated words or symbols. This may help you see missing pieces, understand relationships between parts, and select the right answer.

You will *follow instructions!*

Read and understand the directions. If you're supposed to check off *every* correct answer to each question in a multiple-choice test—and you assume only *one* answer to each question is correct—you're going to omit a lot of answers!

If you're to answer two essay questions out of five, you will probably run out of time if you try to answer all five. And even if you do manage to answer all of them, your teacher will probably only grade the first two. Because you allocated so much time to the other three, it's highly doubtful your first two answers will be detailed and polished enough to earn a good grade.

If there are pertinent facts or formulas you're afraid you'll forget, write them down somewhere in your test booklet before you do anything else. It won't take much time, and it could save you some serious memory jogs later.

Take all the time you need

Don't depend on a wall clock to tell you the time. Bring a watch (but not your phone).

Speaking of time, don't make a habit of leaving tests early. There is little to be gained from supposedly impressing the teacher and other students with how smart you (think you) are by being first to finish. If you are completely satisfied with your answers to all of the questions, it's fine to leave, even if you are first. But in general, slowing down will help you avoid careless mistakes.

Likewise, don't worry about what everybody else is doing. Leave time at the end to recheck your answers. Even if you're the last person left, who cares? Everybody else could have failed, no matter how early and confidently they strode from the room! So take all the time you need and do the best you can.

Attacking multiple-choice tests

There are three ways to attack a multiple-choice test:

1. Start at the first question and keep going, question by question, until you reach the end, never leaving a question until you have either answered it fully or made an educated guess.
2. Answer every *easy* question first—the ones you know the answers to without any thinking at all

or which require the simplest calculations—then
go back and do the harder ones.

3. Answer the *hardest* questions first, and leave the
easy ones to the end.

None of these three options is inherently right or wrong.
Each may work for different individuals. (And I'm assuming
that these three approaches are all in the context of the test
format. Weighted sections may well affect your strategy.)

The first approach is, in one sense, the quickest, in that
no time is wasted reading through the whole test trying to
pick out either the easiest or hardest questions. Presuming
you do not allow yourself to get too stumped by any question,
forcing you to spend an inordinate amount of time on it, it is
probably the method most of you employ.

The second approach ensures that you will maximize
your right answers—you're answering all those you are certain of first. It may also, presuming that you knock off these
easy ones relatively quickly, give you the most time to work on
those that you find particularly vexing.

Many experts recommend this method because they
maintain that answering so many questions one after another
gives you immediate confidence to tackle the questions you're
not sure about. If you find that you agree, then by all means
use this strategy. However, you may consider just *noting* easy
ones as you pre-read the test. This takes less time and, to me,
delivers the same "confidence boost."

The last approach is actually the one I used. In fact, I
made it a point to do the very hardest questions first, then
work my way "down" the difficulty ladder. (This means I
often worked *backward,* since many test makers and teachers
make their tests progressively more difficult.)

This approach may sound strange to you, so let me explain
the psychology. I figured if time pressure started getting to me

at the end of the test, I would rather be in a position to answer the easiest questions—and a lot of them—in the limited time left, rather than ones I really had to think about. After all, by the end of the test, my mind was simply not working as well as it was at the beginning!

That's the major benefit of the third approach: When I was most "up," most awake, most alert, I tackled questions that required the most analysis, thinking, and interpretation. When I was most tired—near the end—I was answering the questions that were virtual "gimmes."

At the same time, I was also giving myself a *real* shot of confidence. As soon as I finished the first hard question, I already felt better. When I finished all of the hard ones, I knew that the rest of the test was all downhill.

I would always, however, try to ensure adequate time to at least answer for every question. Better to get one question wrong and complete three others than get one right and leave three blank.

Don't fall into the "answer daze," that blank stare some students get when they can't think of an answer—for 10 minutes. Do *some*thing. Better to move on and get that one question wrong than waste invaluable time doing nothing.

Play the elimination game

There is usually nothing wrong with guessing, unless, of course, you know wrong answers will be penalized. Even then, the question is how *much* to guess.

If there's no penalty for wrong answers, *never* leave an answer blank. But you should also do everything you can to increase your odds of getting it right. If every multiple-choice question lists four possible answers, you have a 25-percent chance of being right (and, of course, a 75-percent chance of being wrong) each time you have to guess.

But if you can eliminate a single answer—even if you are only reasonably certain it cannot be right—your chances of being correct increase to 33 percent.

And if you can get down to a choice between two answers, the odds are the same as a coin flip: 50-50. In the long run, you will guess as many right as wrong. Even if there is a penalty for guessing, I'd probably pick one answer if I'd reduced the odds to 50-50.

Should you ever change a guess?

How valid was your first guess? Statistics show it was probably pretty darned good (presuming you had some basis for guessing in the first place). So good that you should only change it *if*:

> It really was just a wild guess and, upon further thought, you conclude that answer really should be eliminated (in which case your next guess is, at least, not quite as wild).

> You remembered something that changed the odds of your guess completely (or the answer to a later question helped you figure out the answer to this one).

> You miscalculated on a math problem.

> You misread the question and didn't notice a "not," "never," "always," or similar important qualifier.

What if you eliminate three of the four answers and are convinced that the one that's left—your supposedly "right" answer—is flat-out wrong? Eliminate it and start your analysis all over again with the other three potential answers (one of which, you now believe, *must* be the right one).

If you do guess at any of the objective questions and expect that your test paper will be returned to you, place a little dot or other symbol beside them. That way you will be able to assess how successful your guessing was.

If there is time during a test for you to come back to questions and think about them one more time, go ahead and cross out the answers you know aren't correct. That will simply save you time. You will ignore the answers that are struck out and concentrate on the ones that remain. A small point, but it can save you several seconds per question.

When you think you have finished a whole section, look on the answer sheet or in the blue book to make sure you haven't missed a page.

How to ace any multiple-choice test

> Be careful you don't read too much into questions. Don't try to second-guess the test preparer and look for patterns or tricks that aren't really there.

> A positive choice is more likely to be correct than a negative one.

> Don't go against your first impulse unless you are *sure* you are wrong.

> Check for negatives and other words that are there to throw you off. ("Which of the following is **not**...")

> The answer is usually wrong if it contains "all," "always," "never," or "none." I repeat, usually.

> The answer has a great chance of being right if it contains "sometimes," "probably," or "some."

> When you don't know the right answer, look for the wrong ones.

> Don't eliminate an answer unless you actually know what every word means.

> Read every answer before you pick one (unless you are wildly guessing at the last minute and there's no penalty). Test makers have been known to place a decoy answer that's *almost right* first, just to tempt you to pick it without even reading the other choices.

> On a standardized test, consider transferring all the answers from one section to the answer sheet at the same time.

> The longest and/or most complicated answer to a question is often correct, since the test maker has been forced to add qualifying clauses or phrases to make that answer complete and unequivocal.

> Be suspicious of choices that should be obvious to a two-year-old. Why would the teacher give you such a present? Maybe she didn't.

> Don't give up on a question that, after one reading, seems hopelessly confusing or hard. Looking at it from a different angle, restating it in your own words, or drawing a picture may help you understand it after all.

> If the test maker rarely gives you the option to choose "all of the above" or "none of the above," either may be the correct answer when offered.

> If you are *sure* at least two answers are correct, "all of the above" is the right choice.

> Even if you are only reasonably sure none of the other answers is correct, then "none of the above" may be the right answer.

> ❯   If the question requires a singular answer, elimi-
>   nate all answers that are plural.
> ❯   If the question implies the answer is in the pres-
>   ent tense, confidently eliminate all answers in
>   the past or future tenses.

Reading comprehension questions

This is the kind of test that features a short essay followed
by several questions. You are supposed to find the answers to
those questions in the essay, in which they may be hidden in
one fashion or another.

Here's the method I recommend for answering reading
comprehension questions:

1. Read the questions *before* you read the selection.
    They will alert you to what you're looking for and
    affect the way you read the passage. If dates are
    asked for, circle all dates in the passage as you
    read. If you're looking for facts rather than con-
    clusions, it will, again, change the way you read
    the passage.

2. Or, when you first read the question but before
    you look at the answers, decide what you *think*
    the answer is. If your answer is one of the choices,
    bingo!

3. If the correct answer is not obvious to you, slowly
    read the essay, keeping in mind the questions
    you've just read. Don't underline too much, but
    do underline conjunctions that alter the direction
    of the sentence: "however," "although," "neverthe-
    less," "yet," and so forth. Because of this shift,
    there is a good chance that this sentence will fig-
    ure in one of the questions.

For example: "John Smith was the kind of writer who preferred writing over editing, *while* his wife Lois was interested in the latter over the former," might provide the answer to the question: "Did Lois Smith prefer writing or editing?" A careless glance back at the text will cause you to select "writing" as the answer.

4. Read the questions again. Then go back and forth, uncovering the answer to the first, the second, and so forth. Don't skip around unless the first question is an absolute stumper. If you jump around too much, you'll get confused again and won't answer any of the questions very completely or even correctly.

Mastering multiple-choice math

If you can avoid a calculation, it will save you time. For example, can you figure out the answer to the following problem *without actually doing the math*?

334 x 412 =

(A) 54,559
(B) 137,608
(C) 22,528
(D) 229,766

You can eliminate two of the possible answers just by multiplying the last digits in each number (4 x 2). The answer *must* end in 8. So (A) and (D) have been eliminated...that quickly!

Now, look more carefully at (B) and (C). Can you find the right answer quickly? You need to make an educated guess, known in math circles as "guesstimating." You should be able to multiply 334 x 100 in your head and get 33,400. So (C) *has* to be wrong—it is clearly too small a number. You are left with (B).

Should you do the actual calculation to confirm that (B) is correct? Why would you? You are certain that (A) and (D) are wrong. Absolutely. You know that (C) is much too low. Mark (B) as the answer and move on.

Here are other ways to better your score on math tests:

> Try to figure out what is being asked, what principles are involved, what information is important, and what's not. Don't let extraneous data throw you off track. Make sure you know the *kind* of answer you're seeking: Is it a speed, weight, angle, exponent, or square root?

> Whenever you can, "translate" formulas and numbers into words. Estimate the answer before you even begin the actual calculation. At least you'll know the size of the ballpark you're playing in!

> Even if you're not particularly visual, pictures can often help. Try translating a particularly vexing math problem into a drawing or diagram.

> Play around. There are often different paths to the same solution, even equally valid solutions.

> When you are checking your calculations, try working *backward*. It's an easy way to catch simple arithmetical errors.

> Write down all of your calculations—neatly. You'll be less likely to make a mistake if you take your time, and if you *do* make a mistake, it will be a lot easier to spot.

> Show every step and formula, even if you would normally skip a few. If you knew all of the

principles and formulas but miscalculated near the very beginning of your analysis, you are not going to arrive at the correct answer. *But* many enlightened math teachers will not penalize you too severely if they can clearly see you knew your stuff and did everything right, with the exception of hitting the right button on your calculator.

> If you are using a calculator, double-check your answer immediately. You may enter a wrong number once; the odds against hitting the *same* wrong number a second time are pretty high.

Presuming you've managed to eliminate one or more answers, but are still unsure of the correct answer and have no particular way to eliminate any others, here are some real insider tips to make your guess more "educated":

> If two answers sound alike, choose neither.
> The most "obvious" answer to a difficult question is probably wrong, but an answer that is close to it is probably right.
> If the answers that are left cover a broad range, choose a number in the middle.
> If two quantities are very close, choose one of them.
> If two numbers differ only by a decimal point (and the others aren't close), choose one of them. (Example: 2.3, 40, 1.5, 6, 15; I'd go with 1.5 or 15. If I could at least figure out from the question where the decimal point should go, even better!)
> If two answers *look* alike—either formulas or shapes—choose one of them.

Remember: This is not the way to ace a test—these are just some tried-and-true ways to increase your guessing power when *you have absolutely nothing else to go on and nothing left to do.*

50/50 odds aren't bad. True or false?

What can you do to increase your scores on true-false tests?

First of all, be more inclined to guess if you have to. After all, I encouraged you to guess on a multiple-choice test if you could eliminate enough wrong answers to get down to two, one of which is correct. Well, you're already there! So unless you are being penalized for guessing, guess away! Even if you are being penalized, you may well want to take a shot if you have the faintest clue of the correct answer.

In fact, your odds are often better than 50-50. Most test preparers tend to include more "true" statements than false. So if you really don't have any way to determine the truth of a statement, *presume it is true.* If there is a specific detail in the statement—"There are 206 bones in the adult human body"—it may also tend to be true.

What tricks do test makers incorporate in true-false tests? Here are some to watch out for:

Two parts (statements) that *are* true (or, at least, *may* be true) linked in such a way that the *whole* statement becomes false. Example: "Since many birds can fly, they use stones to grind their food." Many birds *do* fly, and birds *do* swallow stones to grind their food, but a *causal relationship* (the word "since") between the two clauses makes the whole statement false.

On a multiple-choice test, the longest and/or most complicated answer to a question is often correct. The exact *opposite* is true regarding true-false tests: The longer and/or more complicated a statement in a true-false test, the *less* likely it's true since *every clause* of it must be true (and there are so many chances for a single part to be false).

Few broad, general statements are true *without exception*. Pay attention when you see the words "all," "always," "no," "never," or other absolutes. As long as you can think of a *single* example that proves such a statement false, then it is false. But be careful: There are statements with such absolutes that *are* true; they're just rare.

Likewise, words like "sometimes," "often," "frequently," "generally," "usually," "much," "may," "probably," "might," and "ordinarily" make more modest claims and thus usually indicate "true" statements.

Be careful of double negatives: A statement claiming that something is "not uncommon" actually means that it *is* common.

Strategy tip: It's easier for a teacher to add something to make a statement *false.* So when you read the statement, look for anything that will make the whole statement false. If you can't find it, assume it is *true.*

There are no "easy" tests

Some people think "open book" tests are the easiest of all. They pray for them—until they see their first one.

These are the toughest tests of all, if only because even normally "nice" teachers feel no compunction whatsoever about making such tests tougher than a Marine drill instructor. *Heck, you can use your book!* That's like having a legal crib sheet, right? Many open-book tests are also take-home tests, meaning you can use your notes (and any other books or tools you can think of).

Since you have to anticipate that there will be no easy questions, no matter how well you know the material, you need to do some preparation before this type of test:

> Mark important pages by turning down corners, attaching paper clips, or any other method that will help you quickly flip to important charts, tables, summaries, or illustrations.
> Write an index of the pages you've turned down so you know where to find each chart, graph, table, and so forth.
> Summarize all important facts, formulas, etc. on a separate sheet.
> If you are allowed to consult your notes in class or plan to use them during a take-home test, write a brief index of them (general topics only) so you know where to quickly locate pertinent information.

First, answer the questions for which you don't need the textbook. Then work on those questions for which you must rely fully on the book.

Be careful about quoting too freely from your text. Better to make up a similar example rather than use the same one in your book, to paraphrase your text rather than quote it directly, even if you use quotation marks.

While a take-home test is, by definition, an open-book test, it is the hardest of all. An open-book test in class simply can't last longer than the time allotted for the class. But you may be given a night or two, even a week or longer, to complete a take-home exam.

Why are they so hard? You're *given* so much time because teachers expect that it will take you *longer* than the time available in class to finish. You may have to go well beyond your text(s) and notes to even get a handle on some of the questions, leading to some long nights. Take any easy *eight-hour* tests lately? The longer you're given, the easier it is to procrastinate ("Heck, I've got another two nights!"), and we know where *that* leads.

There are only two good aspects to balance the scales. You've certainly been given the chance to "be all that you can be." No excuse for not doing a terrific job on a test with virtually no time limit. And, if you tend to freeze during a normal exam, you should have far less anxiety taking one at home in comfortable surroundings.

Write a prize-winning essay

You need to budget your time for an essay test just as you should for any test—the mathematical calculations are just easier. If you have been instructed to complete three essays in an hour, it doesn't take an Einstein to figure out you should allocate 20 minutes for each.

Or does it? In this example, allow 15 minutes per essay, which will give you 15 minutes to review, proofread, and make corrections and additions to all your answers. And if any of the questions are "weighted" more than the others, adjust the time you spend on them accordingly.

When the time you've budgeted for the first question is up, immediately move on to the next, no matter how far you've gotten on the first. You'll have time at the end—if you follow my suggestion—to go back and add more.

Most teachers will give you a better overall grade for three incomplete but decent essays than for two excellent ones and one left blank.

Don't ever, *ever* begin writing the answer to an essay question without a little "homework" first, even if you're the school's prizewinning journalist.

First, really look at the question. Are you sure you know what it's asking? Put it in your own words and compare it with your teacher's. Do they clearly mean the same thing? If not, you've misread it.

One way to avoid this problem is to paraphrase the question and make it the first sentence of your essay. Even if you have misread the teacher's question, you have shown her how *you* interpreted it. If you answer a slightly different question than the teacher intended, you may still get full credit for a well-written essay.

But please *don't*, intentionally or otherwise, misread the question in such a way that you answer the question you'd *prefer* rather than the one you've actually been given.

Make sure you understand the meaning of the "direction verbs." Don't "describe" when you've been told to "compare and contrast." Don't "explain" when you're supposed to "argue." I've included a list of the most-used verbs and what each is instructing you to do later in this chapter.

A foolproof action plan

Here's the step-by-step way to answer every essay question:

Step one: On a blank sheet of paper, write down all the facts, ideas, concepts, and statistics you feel should be included in your answer.

Step two: Organize them in the order in which they should appear. You don't have to rewrite your notes into a detailed outline—just number each note according to where you want to place it in your essay.

Step three: Compose your first paragraph. It should summarize and introduce the key points you will make in your essay. *This is where superior essay answers are made or unmade.*

Step four: Write your essay, with your penmanship as legible as possible. Most teachers I've known do *not* go out of their way to decipher chicken scratch masquerading as an essay and do *not* award high grades to it either. If you are allowed (encouraged, even required) to use a laptop or tablet, you would avoid this pitfall.

Step five: Reread your essay and, if necessary, add important points you left out, correct spelling and grammar, and polish as much as you can. Also watch for a careless omission that could cause serious damage—leaving out a "not," making the point opposite of the one you intended.

If there is a particular fact you know is important and should be included but you just can't remember it, guess if you can. Otherwise, just leave it out. If the rest of your essay is well-thought-out and organized and clearly communicates all the other points that should be included, I doubt most teachers will mark you down too severely for such an omission.

Don't set yourself up for a poor grade by making guesses you really don't have to. If you think something occurred in 1784, but are afraid it could be 1794, just write "in the late 18th century." You probably will *not* be marked down for the latter phrase, but *may* lose a point or two if you cite a wrong date.

Remember: Few teachers will be impressed by length. A well-organized, well-constructed, specific answer to their question will always get you a better grade than writing down everything you know in the faint hope that you will actually include something pertinent. Writing a superior essay on the little you do know will usually earn you a better grade than knowing a lot and presenting it poorly.

Common Instructional Verbs on Essay Tests

Compare   Examine two or more objects, ideas, people, etc., and note similarities and differences.

Contrast   Compare to highlight differences. Similar to *differentiate*, *distinguish*.

Criticize   Judge and discuss merits and faults. Similar to *critique*.

Define   Explain the nature or essential qualities.

Describe   Convey appearance, nature, attributes, etc.

Discuss   Consider or examine by argument, comment, etc.; debate; explore solutions.

Enumerate   List various events, things, descriptions, ideas, etc.

Evaluate   Appraise the worth of an idea, comment, etc., and justify your conclusion.

Explain   Make the meaning of something clear, plain, intelligible, and/or understandable.

Illustrate   Use specific examples or analogies to explain.

Interpret   Give the meaning of something by paraphrase, by translation, or by an explanation based on personal opinion.

Justify   Defend a statement or conclusion. Similar to *support*.

Narrate	Recount the occurrence of something, usually by giving details of events in the order in which they occurred. Similar to *describe*, but only applicable to something that happens in time.
Outline	Do a general sketch, account, or report, indicating only the main features of a book, subject, or project.
Prove	Establish the truth or genuineness by evidence or argument. Similar to *show*, *explain*, *demonstrate*. (In math, verify validity by mathematical demonstration.)
Relate	Give an account of events and/or circumstances, usually to establish association, connections, or relationships.
Review	Survey a topic, occurrence, or idea, generally but critically. Similar to *describe*, *discuss*, *illustrate*, *outline*, *summarize*, *trace*. Some test-makers may use these words virtually interchangeably, although one can find subtle differences in each.
State	Present the facts concisely and clearly. May be used interchangeably with *name*, *list*, *indicate*, *identify*, *enumerate*, *cite*.
Summarize	State in concise form, omitting examples and details.
Trace	Follow the course or history of an occurrence, idea, etc.

Worry less about the specific words and more about the information. Organize your answer to a fault and write to be understood, not to impress. Better to use shorter sentences, paragraphs, and words—and be clear and concise—than to let the teacher fall into a clausal nightmare from which he may never emerge (and neither will your A!).

If you don't have the faintest clue what the question means, ask. If you still have no idea of the answer—and I mean *zilch*—leave it blank. Better to allocate more time to other parts of the test and do a better job on those.

Take time at the end of the test to review not only your essay answers but your other answers as well. Make sure all words and numbers are readable. Make sure you have matched the right question to the right answer. Even make sure you didn't miss a whole section by turning over a page too quickly or not noticing that a page was missing. Make sure you can't, simply *can't*, add anything more to any of the essay answers.

What if time runs out?

While you should have carefully allocated sufficient time to complete each essay before you started working on the first, things happen. You may find yourself with two minutes left and one essay to go. What do you do? As quickly as possible, write down every piece of information you think should be included, and number each point in the order you would have written it. If you then have time to reorganize your notes into a clearer outline, do so. Many teachers will give you at least partial credit if your outline contains all the information the answer was supposed to. It will at least show you knew a lot about the subject and were capable of outlining a reasonable response.

One of the reasons you may have left yourself with insufficient time to answer one or more questions is that you knew too darned much about the previous question(s). And you wanted to make sure the teacher *knew* you knew, so you wrote...and wrote...and wrote...until you ran out of time.

Be careful—some teachers throw in a relatively general question that you could conceivably write about until next Wednesday. In that case, they aren't testing your knowledge of the whole subject as much as your ability to *edit* yourself, to organize and summarize the *important* points.

Alphabet soup tests

The various standardized tests used in college and graduate school admissions—the SAT, ACT, LSAT, GRE, and others—require their own pointers. These, like my oral exams at the end of four years of college, are not specific to any course or even one grade. Rather, they are attempting to assess your ability to apply mathematical concepts, read and understand various passages, and demonstrate language skills.

The three-and-a-half-hour ACT consists of 200-plus multiple-choice questions divided into four sections—English, math, reading, and science—plus an optional 40-minute writing test. It bills itself as an "achievement test," characterizing the SAT as an "aptitude test."

The College Board is unveiling a redesigned version of the three-hour SAT that will be administered for the first time in 2016, reverting back to its previous 1600-point scale (800 each for reading and math sections), making the 50-minute essay optional. It is also producing new PSAT exams for 10th and 11th graders around the same time.

The SAT penalizes you for guessing. The ACT does not.

Despite their ephemeral nature, you *can* study for standardized tests by practicing. A solid review of English and math is essential. If you think geometry is just for squares, you'd better change your tune!

There are a variety of companies specializing in preparing students for each of these tests—your school might even sponsor its own course—and many bookstores contain a wide selection of massive preparation guides.

You may consider investing the time and money in any such reputable course—such as Stanley Kaplan, Princeton Review, BAR/BRI—or, at the very least, buying one of the major test-prep books.

Because these are, indeed, *standard*ized tests, learning and utilizing specific techniques pertinent to them and practicing on previous tests *can* significantly increase your scores, if only because you will feel less anxious and have a better idea of what's in store for you.

There are students who achieve exceptional test scores on the SAT or ACT and go on to compile barely adequate college records. These people are said to "test well": The testing environment doesn't throw them and they have sufficient prior experience to have an edge on the rest of the competition. Others "choke" during such tests but wind up at the top of the career pyramid.

You've probably been told for most of your life that your score on the SAT or ACT will determine whether you are a raving success eating in the finest restaurants or the busboy that cleans up afterward. How vital are these scores to the college admission process and, one presumes, to the rest of your life? Still important, but not necessarily to the college *you* want to attend.

More than 850 colleges—a surprisingly large number though still a substantial minority of the collegiate universe—no longer even require the SAT or ACT for admission.

Though one method of predicting success, such tests are not, by any means, perfect oracles. Nor are their conclusions inalienable. Many people have succeeded in life without doing particularly well on standardized tests.

Important note: Many standardized tests are offered only on computer (CAT—for computer-adaptive testing format). Among the most important that fall into this category are the GMAT (Graduate Management Admissions Test), GRE (Graduate Record Exam), and TOEFL (Test of English as a Foreign Language), along with a number of specific licensing tests. (But not the SAT or ACT, at least for now.)

What does this mean to you? Tests available only in CAT format require a different strategy because of two important factors: You can't return to a previous answer, and you can't skip a question and return to it later. Make sure you know if you are taking a computer or written test and practice (and strategize) accordingly!

A special note for parents

Many parents take their children's grades and test scores far too seriously. Here's my advice to them:

> Don't get overanxious about your child's test scores. Overemphasizing grades can upset a child, especially one already chafing under too much pressure.

> Children who are afraid of failing are more likely to make mistakes on tests. Help them feel confident about everything they do.

> Don't judge your child by a single test score, no matter how important the test. No test is a perfect measure of what a child can do or what she has actually learned.

> Talk to your child's teacher as often as possible. Her assessment will be a far better measure of how your child is doing than any test, even a series of tests.

> Make sure your child attends school regularly. He can't do well on tests if he is rarely in class.

> Make sure your child gets enough sleep, especially before a big test. A tired mind leads to tired grades.

> Review test results with your child and show him what he can learn from a graded exam paper. This is especially crucial in math and the sciences, where each new concept builds upon the previous ones.

> Look at the *wrong* answers. Find out why she answered as she did. This may identify times when your child knew the right answer but didn't fully understand the question.

> Read and discuss any teacher comments on the test, especially if your child received a poor grade.

Pretest Organizer

Class: _____   **Teacher:** _____

Test date: _____   **Time:** From: _____ To: _____

Place: _____

Special instructions to myself (e.g., take calculator, dictionary, etc.):

_____
_____
_____
_____
_____
_____

Materials I need to study for this test (check all needed):
_____ Book   _____ DVDs/videos
_____ Workbook   _____ Old tests
_____ Class notes   _____ Other
_____ Handouts

Format of the test (write the number of T/F, essays, and so forth, and total points for each section):

_____
_____
_____
_____
_____
_____

Study group meetings (times, places):

1. _____

2. _____

3. _____

4. _____

5. _____

6. _____

7. _____

8. _____

Material to be covered:

Indicate topics, sources, and amount of review (light or heavy) required. Check when review is completed.

Topic	Sources	Review
_____	_____	_____
_____	_____	_____
_____	_____	_____
_____	_____	_____
_____	_____	_____
_____	_____	_____
_____	_____	_____
_____	_____	_____
_____	_____	_____

After the test:
Grade I expected _____ Grade I received _____

What did I do that helped me?

_____

_____

_____

_____

_____

_____

_____

_____

_____

What else should I have done?

_____

_____

_____

_____

_____

_____

_____

_____

_____

Celebrate your Success

I'm proud of you. You made it all the way through the book. Here's my final advice:

> Reread *How to Study,* cover to cover. It's just like seeing a movie for the second time—you always find something you missed the first time around.

> Practice what I preached. You had an *excuse* for flunking before—you didn't know how to study. Now you have absolutely *no* excuse.

> Write me a letter or email me to tell me what particular advice helped you and how much better you're doing in school.

Write me:

Ron Fry
c/o Career Press
12 Parish Drive
Wayne, NJ 07470

Or email me: Ronfry@careerpress.com

I promise I will try to respond if you ask, but please don't call—I'll probably be somewhere promoting *How to Study!*

INDEX